Fish Out Of Wa

A Comedy

Derek Benfield

Samuel French – London
New York – Sydney – Toronto – Hollywood

This is the original 1963 version of *Fish Out of Water*. A revised version, published in 1986, is also available. The ISBN is 0 573 11187 1 and the cast is M3 F4.

Fish Out Of Water

This play was first produced at the New Theatre, Bromley, on 2nd April 1962 with the following cast:

BRIGADIER HUBBACK	Robert Lankesheer
MRS. HUBBACK	Zulema Dene
MARISA	Sheila Barker
DORA COWLEY	Rosemary Frankau
AGATHA HEPWORTH	Rose Power
FIONA FRANCIS	Carmen Hill
MR. MALLET	Peter Goss
JULIAN WHITTLE	Aidan Turner
LEN BARRETT	Tony Holland

Produced by DAVID POULSON

Setting by GLEN EDWARDS

The scene throughout is the lounge of an hotel on the Italian Riviera.

ACT ONE

Afternoon of a hot summer's day

ACT TWO

SCENE 1	The following morning, after breakfast
SCENE 2	Before lunch, the same day

ACT THREE

After dinner, the same evening

No character in this play is intended to portray any specific person, alive or dead.

Running time of this play, excluding intervals, is approximately one hour and fifty minutes.

COPYRIGHT INFORMATION

PRODUCTION NOTE

FISH OUT OF WATER takes place in a sun-drenched hotel somewhere on the Italian Riviera. The sort of romantic, sweet-smelling spot we all long to escape to for a little peace and quiet after the bustle of London or Manchester or whatever. There are flowers everywhere, the sun is hot and the sea is crystal clear and beautifully blue. Into this idyllic setting strides Agatha Hepworth, a loud, outspoken, jovial cockney widow, and her timid, spinster sister, Fiona Francis. Agatha, rosy and beaming crushes all protests as she rounds up the hotel guests into communal games and joint enterprises of every kind. They came on holiday, she maintains, to enjoy themselves—and *she* is going to see that they do! With untiring energy she invades the private lives of all the characters with surprising and riotous results.

Fish Out of Water is a comedy, not a farce. The people are all real people, and what happens to them are the sort of things that could (and do) happen to us all on a holiday abroad. We have all met Agatha somewhere. However far you travel, be it Brittany or the Balkans, she somehow always manages to be there. In playing her, make sure you give her plenty of light and shade; find the places where you can drop the attack or she may become monotonous. And remember that Agatha is, in the main, a *happy* woman and must not be played as a stern-faced harridan. She is bubbling over with joy—a joy she is willing, or rather determined, to communicate to others.

Fiona Francis, on the other hand, is subdued and pessimistic. She has come on holiday very much against her will and sees disaster round every corner—that is, until she meets Love on the Beach in the person of Mr. Mallet. Fiona has an endearing quality, and she and Agatha provide excellent foils for each other.

The other characters are varied and offer plenty of scope to a good company. Julian Whittle, for instance, who has had enough of Italians, sunshine and, most of all, tiresome English tourists, is the local representative of a travel agency through which (unfortunately for him) Agatha and Fiona have booked. He has a dry sense of humour and a long-suffering manner. Throughout the play he gets progressively more and more exhausted, and there is a lot of fun to be had out of his dilemma.

Mr. Mallet from the bank in Brighton is a bewildered little man who has somehow become separated from the rest of his coach party and whose high hopes of Continental travel have gone sour on him, but who eventually finds consolation in the arms of Fiona. Brigadier and Mrs. Hubback want only to be left alone to enjoy the sunshine that used to be reserved for the rich; or at least they *think* they do, until the Brigadier finds authority again in organizing a country-wide search for a missing tourist, and his wife remembers a long-forgotten talent for cricket. These two parts are very rewarding, but do not play him as too much of a buffoon, or her too much of a prig.

Dora Cowley is a bus conductress from Oldham and should have a decided North Country burr. She is by no means glamorous (we must know why Len prefers the Italian girl), but has a lovable quality of helplessness. There is a parallel between her and Fiona (as seen in Act Two, p.43); both spinsters, one young and hopeful, the other older and resigned. It is only at the end of the play that the "transformation" takes place and Cinderella goes off to the Ball.

Len Barrett is a bright, effervescent young cockney who has come on holiday for the "birds", but only seems to find Agatha. It is essential that he be played with charm and that we should immediately like him or we shall not be in accord with Dora's feelings for him. The only remaining character is Marisa. Dark, vivacious, and as Italian as can be!

The setting for the play should reflect as far as possible the description in my opening paragraph. The more luxurious and relaxing the setting, the greater the effect when Agatha and Fiona appear.

DEREK BENFIELD

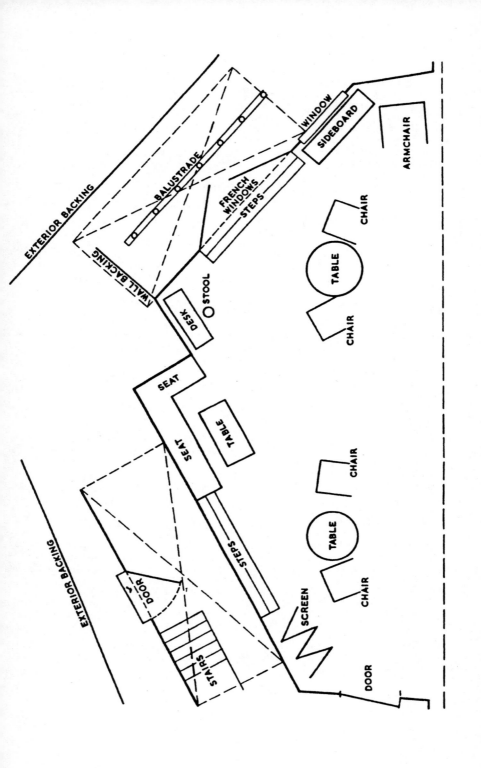

FISH OUT OF WATER

ACT ONE

The lounge of an hotel on the Italian Riviera.
The main entrance is from an archway down two steps U.R.C., *beyond which can be seen the start of the staircase leading up and off to the* R. *and the door to the street. There is a way below the staircase which leads to the proprietor's office, etc. Two further steps at an angle* U.L.C. *lead up to the french windows which open on to a palm-bedecked terrace beyond which is the sea. Below the french windows is another smaller window, and a door* D.R. *leads to the dining-room, kitchen and bar. In the corner* U.C. *is a padded seat with a table in front of it. There are two other tables, one* L.C. *and the other* R.C., *each with chairs* L. *and* R. *of it. There is also a chair in the corner* D.L. *Other furniture, dressing and electrical fittings at the discretion of the producer. There is a bell-push* D.L.

It is afternoon on a day in summer and the sun is scorching down outside. MRS. HUBBACK *is asleep in the wicker arm-chair* R. *of table* L.C *After a moment her husband,* BRIGADIER HUBBACK, *bustles in from the archway carrying a bathing-towel. He is wearing a tropical suit. He crosses to her.*

HUBBACK. Four o'clock, my dear!

(She wakes with a start.)

MRS. H. What about it?
HUBBACK. Thought I might go down to the beach.
MRS. H. Whatever for? It's far too hot.
HUBBACK. I'd like to get a bit brown before I go back. I shall feel jolly silly coming all the way to Italy and going back white. Chap I know got sunburnt at Eastbourne last year. Came back looking like a Hindu.
MRS. H. Nobody sunbathes in the afternoon out here, Charles. They all sleep.
HUBBACK. All right, I tell you what—let's pop down to the village and get a cup of tea. It's quite shady there. Place I saw this morning called itself Ye Olde English Tea Room. Might be worth investigating.

MRS. H. I'd rather stay here.

HUBBACK. But they don't serve tea in the hotel.

MRS. H. I think they will in future. I've been talking to Mario in the kitchen.

HUBBACK. You won't get far with him. He doesn't understand English.

MRS. H. I think he understood me. I spoke very loudly. If not, you must remember I did bring my own kettle.

HUBBACK. You can't very well brew up in the bedroom!

MRS. H. Well, they wouldn't let me in the kitchen.

HUBBACK. I do feel—when in Rome and all that.

MRS. H. Precisely. And that's why I shall continue to doze for as long as the natives do. (*She settles herself to sleep again.*)

> (HUBBACK *sighs, puts down his bathing-things on corner seat* U.C. *as* MARISA *comes in from the dining-room* D.R. *She is a strikingly pretty Italian girl with a good figure. She carries some flowers which she puts in a vase on table* R.C. HUBBACK *brightens considerably as he sees her.*)

HUBBACK (*whispering*). Ah, Marisa! (*Takes a look at* MRS. H., *then crosses eagerly to* MARISA.) Almost tea-time, isn't it?

MARISA (*whispering*). I will bring it now.

HUBBACK (*whispering*). You will? Oh, good. Lovely day.

MARISA (*whispering*). Yes. I have just been to the beach. You will go for a bathe?

MRS. H. He'll do nothing of the sort.

HUBBACK. Thought you were dozing, m'dear.

MARISA. I will bring tea.

MRS. H. If you please.

> (MARISA *goes out* D.R. *He watches her go with undisguised enthusiasm.*)

HUBBACK. Pretty little thing.

MRS. H. Yes, you would notice that. (*He quickly conceals his approval of* MARISA *and shrugs off towards the french windows.*) I don't know what's the matter with you men. The temperature goes above eighty and you all become quite impossible.

> (DORA COWLEY *comes in from the archway* U.R. *She is fair, about 23, and speaks with a North Country dialect. She is not by any means pretty, but there is an appealing quality of helplessness about her.*)

DORA. Oh, hullo, Brigadier! (*He quickly indicates* MRS. H. *and* DORA *instantly becomes more subdued.*) Hullo, Mrs. Hubback.

MRS. H. Good afternoon.

HUBBACK. Going for a swim?

DORA. I might later. Rather sunbathe, really.

HUBBACK (*moving down* L. *of table* L.C.). How's your friend?

DORA (U.R.C.). Rene? She's still terrible. The minute she set foot here she went down like ninepence. It's the food, y'know. Well, it's not like what you get back home, is it? (*Sits chair* R. *of table* R.C.) You'd think they'd consider what we're used to, wouldn't you? You know, sort of cater more for the tourists.

HUBBACK (*good-humouredly*). If you'd wanted fish and chips you should have stayed in England.

DORA. Oh, I quite like it all. But poor Rene—one mouthful of dinner that first evening and off to her room she went. And do you know, she's had nothing but chicken noodle soup ever since!

(MARISA *returns from* D.R. *with a tray of tea-things which she puts down on the table* L.C.)

MARISA (*as she crosses*). I hope you will find everything all right.

HUBBACK. I'm sure we will. Here, let me help you.

MRS. H. (*without looking at him*). It's all right, Charles. She can manage.

(HUBBACK *shrugs at* MARISA, *who smiles sympathetically.* MRS. H. *looks at them and he quickly turns on innocence and sits* L. *of table* L.C.)

MARISA (*to* L. *of* DORA). You would like some tea, miss?

DORA. No, thanks. Not for me.

MARISA. How is your friend? She is better, I hope?

DORA. I'm afraid not.

MARISA. What shall I get her for dinner tonight?

DORA. Chicken noodle, I suppose.

(MARISA *goes off* D.R. MRS. H. *takes lid off the teapot, examines the tea without enthusiasm and stirs it vigorously. During the next few lines she is pouring tea, etc.*)

You been out here before?

HUBBACK. Not Italy. We usually go to France.

DORA. You mean you go every year?

HUBBACK. Most years, yes. (*He takes up a biscuit, but* MRS. H. *slaps his hand and he drops it.*)

DORA. This is my first time. We've got a scheme now at our depot.

HUBBACK. Your—depot?

DORA. Yes. I'm a clippie.

HUBBACK. A what?

DORA. A bus conductress.

HUBBACK. Good heavens! I've never met a bus conductress before. I mean, I've never seen one without her uniform on. (MRS. H. *gives him a weary look.*) Oh, you know what I mean!

DORA. We all pay in so much a week. It's ever such a good idea. You ought to try it. As soon as I get back I start all over again.

HUBBACK. Well, I wonder what the new intake will be like. Quite a few went home after lunch, so there should be some more arriving this afternoon.

MRS. H. If they're anything like the ones who left they'll be frightful. That man from Cleethorpes had the loudest laugh I've ever heard.

DORA. It's awful the first day you arrive, isn't it? Everyone staring at you as you come into the dining-room.

HUBBACK. Well, we're all a bit shy at first, y'know. Natural English reticence. Rather nice, I think.

(Gets a stony look from his wife.)

During the past ten days I've seen a lot of 'em come and go, y'know. It's wonderful to see them arrive— all white and tired and sheepish. They come in through that door so timidly, as if they'd no right to be here. *(Sound of voices outside.)* Hullo, that sounds like someone! *(He rises and moves above table L.C.)* You watch 'em as they come in and you'll see what I mean. Hardly speak above a whisper.

(AGATHA HEPWORTH appears in the open doorway. She is a cheerful cockney woman of about 45. She has a loud voice and is beaming with joy.)

AGATHA. This is the 'otel Floreat?

HUBBACK. Er—yes, it is.

AGATHA *(shouting off)*. All right, Fiona, this is it!

(She advances into the room, beaming with delight as she takes in her new surroundings. She is wearing a thick tweed suit and a hat, and carries a week-end case and a handbag.)

(To the room in general.) Oh, it's lovely, isn't it? Just like the picture in the brotcher.

HUBBACK *(moving to L. of AGATHA)*. Er—good afternoon.

AGATHA. Good afternoon. 'ere you are—you'd better take that. *(Hands HUBBACK her case.)* There are some more outside. Fiona's just seeing to them. *(To the door to call.)* Fiona! What are you doing? Come on in 'ere! *(She returns to the astonished HUBBACK.)* She's so slow. Doesn't know if it's pancake Tuesday or Maffeking night. I expect you'll want to see my passport and so on?

HUBBACK. Well—

AGATHA. No? You're the first one who's said that. All the way 'ere, nothing but passport out, passport away. I could 'ave a whole arsenal amongst my luggage, but as long as my passport's all right everyone's 'appy! Marvellous, isn't it? *(To the door again.)* What's she doing out there? Fiona! Just bring the luggage inside. You don't 'ave to unpack it on the pavement! (*Returns to the* BRIGADIER *again.*)

HUBBACK. Mrs.—er—

AGATHA. 'Epworth. Agatha 'Epworth. British subject.

HUBBACK. Yes, but—

AGATHA. Oh, I'm sorry! I forgot! You don't speak English. Silly of me. (*Elocuting and gesturing.*) What—is—the—number—of—my room? Number—of—room?

      (HUBBACK *gazes at her in amazement, and she takes out a phrasebook and thumbs through it.*)

Che numero—ha la mia camera?

HUBBACK. No, no, no! I—

AGATHA. Don't tell me you 'aven't got any rooms!

HUBBACK. No, no!

AGATHA. Well, you'll 'ave to find one, won't you? 'ere I am and 'ere I stay! (*Consults phrase-book.*) *Ecco-mi fermero!* I've got my little pink form and that's all I need.

MRS. H. Mrs. Hepworth, this is my husband.

AGATHA. Your 'usband? You mean you're not—

HUBBACK. I'm staying here.

AGATHA. Oh, I'm ever so sorry. How could I do a thing like that! Do forgive me. 'ere, you'd better give me that back. (*Makes to take back her case.*)

HUBBACK. It's quite all right. I'll put it down here. (*Puts down the case* U.C.)

AGATHA. Thank you. That is kind. (*To* MRS. H.) You must think I'm awful.

      (MRS. H. *gives her a look that does not either confirm or deny.*)

HUBBACK (*dropping down to above table* L.C.). Not at all. My name is Hubback. Brigadier Hubback. And this is my wife.

AGATHA. Brigadier! Well, I never! And I thought you were—(*Laughs loudly and advances on* MRS. H.) How do you do, Mrs. Hubback? I'm ever so pleased to meet you. (*She shakes her hand vigorously.*)

MRS. H. (*icily*). How do you do?

AGATHA (*seeing* DORA *and crossing to her*). And you must be Miss Hubback. I shouldn't wonder!

DORA. Er—no—er—actually—

MRS. H. This young lady simply happens to be staying here.

AGATHA. There I go again, putting my foot right in it.

DORA. My name's Dora Cowley.

AGATHA. Hullo, Dora. I say, you're ever so brown. Doesn't she look nice?

HUBBACK (*beaming*). She certainly does!

MRS. H. Charles!

> (HUBBACK *retires to* D.L. *suitably subdued.*)

AGATHA. You just in the middle of tea? I came at the right time, didn't I? Where's she got to? (*To door.*) Fiona! (*Returning to* C.) At this rate she'll get 'ere just in time to go 'ome again!

> (*There is a slight pause and then* FIONA FRANCIS *comes in through the door. She is cockney and pessimistic, and has obviously come on holiday very much against her will. She is about 40, and is laden down with two suitcases, a grip, a carrier bag, a brown-paper parcel and an umbrella. She comes slowly to* R. *of* AGATHA.)

Well—whatever took you so long?

FIONA. I'm sorry, Agatha. I was collecting the cases.

AGATHA. You took your time about it. Well, don't stand there holding them in your arms. What are you trying to do—hatch them?

FIONA. What shall I do with them?

AGATHA (*patiently*). Put them down somewhere.

HUBBACK. Here, let me help you.

FIONA. Oh, thank you.

> (HUBBACK *crosses below* MRS. H. *up to* R. *of* FIONA *and helps her to put her things down* U.L. *of the archway.* AGATHA *watches* FIONA *with patient tolerance.*)

HUBBACK. The girl will be back in a moment, then she'll have them moved up to your rooms.

FIONA. Thank you.

AGATHA. You'd better come and sit down.

FIONA. Yes, I will. I'm quite exhausted. (*She sits* L. *of table* R.C.)

AGATHA. I don't know why. You've done nothing all day. This is my sister, Fiona. The kind gentleman over there is Colonel Hubback.

HUBBACK (*as he passes above* AGATHA *to the french windows*). Er— Brigadier, actually.

AGATHA. Sorry—of course, Brigadier. And this is 'is wife.

HUBBACK } (*together*). How do you do?
MRS. H.

FIONA. How do you do?

AGATHA. And over there's Dora Cowley.

DORA. Hullo! (*Rising.*) I'll go and find Marisa. I expect you'd like some tea.

AGATHA. Thank you, love. That would be nice.

> (DORA *goes off* D.R.)

Well, we got 'ere, eh, Fiona?

FIONA. Yes, thank 'eaven. I'm surprised I'm all in one piece.

AGATHA. Now don't be like that. She's done nothing but grumble all the way 'ere.

FIONA. It took such a long time on the train.

AGATHA. What did you expect me to do—get out and push it? I told you we ought to fly, but you wouldn't.

HUBBACK (*dropping down* L.). Why not? It's much quicker, y'know.

FIONA. It ain't safe.

AGATHA. You're the one who ain't safe. You ought to be kept in a cage. (*To above table* R.C.)

> (DORA *returns with* MARISA. *She remains* D.R. *and* MARISA *crosses to below chair* R. *of table* R.C.)

DORA. Here she is, Mrs. Hepworth.

AGATHA. Thank you, dear.

MARISA. *Buon giorno.* Welcome to the Hotel Floreat. We are very glad to have you stay with us.

FIONA (*to* AGATHA, *moved*). Oh, there! Isn't that nice? (*To* MARISA.) Thank you, dear. It's very sweet of you to say so. I must say you know how to be polite here anyway. (*To* AGATHA.) Wasn't it a sweet thing to say, Agatha? "We are very glad to have you stay with us." I do think that was nice. I really do.

AGATHA. All right, all right! You don't 'ave to go raving mad! I don't know. For three hours in the coach you've said nothing, and now all of a sudden you can't stop.

MARISA. I have ordered some tea for you. Afterwards I will show you to your room.

AGATHA. Thank you, dear. (*Consults phrase-book.*) *Grazie.*

MARISA (*with a smile*). *Prego.* Do you have your form from the agency, please?

AGATHA. The pink one? Oh, yes, I've got it 'ere. (*Looks in handbag.*) Got so many bits and pieces 'ere—Passport, no—Rail tickets, no—Itinerary, no—Now where 'ave I put it? (*Suddenly fixes her gaze on* FIONA.) Fiona! You've got it!

FIONA (*cowering*). No, Agatha, I haven't!

AGATHA. I distinctly remember I gave it to you.

FIONA. No, you didn't. You said you couldn't trust me with it. It was just after we'd fixed up about the insurance. We were getting on to the train and you said, "I'd better have that, Fiona, in case anything 'appens to you".

AGATHA (*round to* L. *of* FIONA). Where is it?

FIONA. I haven't got it, Agatha—!

AGATHA. Well, if you 'aven't got it you may as well start going 'ome now!

FIONA (*proffering her bag*). Look, there's nothing 'ere—!

> (AGATHA looks in FIONA's bag. *She produces a pink slip of paper.*)

AGATHA (*glaring at* FIONA). What's this, then? Your birth certificate? (*Crosses below table to* MARISA.) There we are, dear.

MARISA. *Grazie.*

AGATHA. Oh—er—what was that you said just now?

MARISA (*laughing*). *Prego.*

AGATHA. Eh?

HUBBACK. It's like saying "Don't mention it".

AGATHA. I see. Well—prego, then, dear.

> (MARISA *goes off* D.R., *taking the pink form.* AGATHA *is below chair* R. *of table* R.C.)

FIONA. I didn't remember that I'd got it.

AGATHA. I should think you didn't.

FIONA. I never thought.

AGATHA. That's nothing new.

MRS. H. Is your husband coming on later, Mrs. Hepworth?

AGATHA. I 'ope not.

MRS. H. Why?

AGATHA. He's dead. (*She sits* R. *of table* R.C., *takes off a shoe and caresses her foot.*)

MRS. H. Oh, dear. I'm sorry.

AGATHA. No need to be. He was a mean old skinflint was my Harold. If he could get out of paying he would—and did. As a result, when he died he left a sackful. And he left it all to me. Best day's work he ever did. That's why me and Fiona's come out 'ere. If he knew how I was spending his money he'd turn in his grave!

FIONA. So I should think. Waste of money, I call it.

AGATHA. And I don't want you starting that again!

FIONA. I didn't want to come out 'ere in the first place.

AGATHA. Then why did you?

FIONA. What's wrong with Eastcliffe?

AGATHA. I'll tell you what's wrong with Eastcliffe. It's common! That's what it is—common! Same old faces year after year till I got sick of it. We've come 'ere for a change, Fiona Francis—to get away from it all.

MRS. H. Yes, that was the reason I came.

AGATHA. And you were right, Mrs. Hubback. You were right!

FIONA. I knew a woman went abroad once. She was bitten by a bug. They brought 'er back in a box.

AGATHA. You're a little ray of sunshine, aren't you?

DORA (*to above table* R.C.). You'll like it here. It's ever so nice. It's a lovely sandy beach.

FIONA. What about the food?

DORA. Well, it's not like you get in England.

FIONA. I'm not eating none of them octopuses!

AGATHA. You don't get octopuses 'ere! Really, can't you even read the brotcher! Octopuses is Spain!

FIONA. I bet you can't tell what you're eating half the time. If they eat frog's legs in France, 'eaven knows what we'll get 'ere!

AGATHA. You're not going to get anything like that.

FIONA. How can I be sure? I bet you they'll disguise it.

AGATHA. Well, if they disguise it you won't know, will you?

FIONA. I may not know, but my stomach soon will!

AGATHA. After twenty years of your shepherd's pie I reckon your stomach's ready for anything.

DORA. It's what I call rich cooking. You know what I mean? Spices and oil and that sort of thing.

HUBBACK. And there's a lot of pasta, naturally.

FIONA. I'm not 'aving none of them!

AGATHA. Oh, do be quiet. You make me tired.

DORA. The first few days are a bit tricky. But I expect you've brought your Alka-Seltzer. (*Away up to seat* U.C., *where she sits and glances at a magazine.*)

FIONA. My what?

AGATHA. Now don't encourage 'er, Dora. She's bad enough, 'eaven knows.

FIONA. You mean I'm going to be ill?

(FIONA *is goggling.*)

AGATHA. Oh, look, now you've set 'er off!

(MARISA *comes in with a tray of tea for two which she puts down on table* R.C.)

HUBBACK. Have a nice cup of tea. You'll feel fine after that.

FIONA. I don't know that I want any tea. I think I'd like to go to my room—(*Starts to rise.*)

AGATHA (*the voice of thunder*). You'll 'ave some tea and like it! (FIONA *sits again.* AGATHA *turns to* MARISA *with a sweet smile.*) Thank you, dear, that's lovely. *Grazie.*

(MARISA *goes off upstairs, taking some of the baggage with her from* U.C.

AGATHA *pours milk and then proceeds to pour the tea. It is very weak and she shakes the pot around and tries again. She pours from cup to cup and back again, N.A.A.F.I.-wise. She hands a cup to* FIONA.)

'ere you are, Fiona. You can't complain about that.

FIONA (*pessimistically*). I 'aven't tasted it yet.

AGATHA (*producing tea bag from inside the pot*). Well, it's Tetley's Tea Bags the same as you 'ave at 'ome, so get on with it!

FIONA. What's this in little packets? (*Holding up a cellophane package.*)

AGATHA. Sugar, of course. What do you think?

FIONA. All wrapped up like that? Well, I never. They never have it like that in the Kardomah.

AGATHA. Seems a nice 'otel, I must say. Very friendly. I'm all for that —a nice, friendly atmosphere where we can all be one big 'appy family!

(MRS. H. *rises.*)

MRS. H. If you'll excuse me, I think I'll go up to my room.

AGATHA. Yes, of course we'll excuse you, dear.

HUBBACK. How about going down for a bathe, m'dear?

MRS. H. Not now, Charles.

HUBBACK. It's lovely out.

MRS. H. Then we'll go for a walk. I'll be ready in a moment. (*Makes for the archway.*)

HUBBACK. Righto. I'll wait here for you.

(*He gets a look from* MRS. H. *and follows her off obediently.*
AGATHA *looks at* FIONA, *who is still gazing at her tea without drinking it.*)

AGATHA. What are you waiting for? The starting-gun?

FIONA. I don't know if I ought to.

AGATHA. A cuppa tea won't 'urt you.

FIONA. Are you sure it's all right?

AGATHA. 'course it's all right! What do you think they do out 'ere— poison you? Get on with it.

FIONA. Do you think I ought to take this pill now?

AGATHA. That's for travel sickness. You was supposed to take that before you left!

(*From the french windows a small, troubled little man comes in nervously.*
He is of indeterminate middle age and his name is MR. MALLET. *He comes to* U.L.C. *and as he is unnoticed he coughs gently.* FIONA *and* AGATHA *turn in unison to look at him.*)

MALLET. Excuse me. Are you Progressive?

AGATHA. I beg your pardon?

MALLET. Are you with Progressive Tours?

AGATHA. Oh, no. I'm Eagle.

MALLET. Oh, dear. (*Indicating* FIONA.) And your—er—?

AGATHA. She's my sister and she's not progressive at all.

MALLET. And—er—this young lady?

DORA. I'm Universal!

MALLET. Oh, dear.

DORA. What's the matter?

MALLET. They've lost me.

AGATHA. 'oo 'ave?

MALLET. Progressive Tours. I thought I might find them here. (*Coming nearer.*) You see, we were in a coach—thirty-five of us— and we stopped at Monte Carlo. The driver said to meet again at seven-thirty, but when I got back I found they'd gone without me. I've been following them ever since.

AGATHA. That is 'ard luck. Are you sure you didn't make a mistake about the time?

MALLET. No, never! I work at the bank in Brighton. I've been planning this holiday for months, and now this happens. It was silly, wasn't it? Wasn't it silly? See! I've got all the details here. (*Takes out a sheaf of papers and thrusts them at* AGATHA.) This is my itinerary. It's all quite clear. We meet at Victoria at 22.15 on the Tuesday— Depart Victoria 22.45—arrive Newhaven—

AGATHA. Yes, I'm sure that's very interesting.

MALLET. See—I've ticked off each timing as we went along. I'm like that, you see—methodical. And everything was going just like clockwork. And then all of a sudden—Monte Carlo and disaster. It was silly, wasn't it. Wasn't it silly?

AGATHA. I'm sure it's very inconvenient.

MALLET. It's not just the inconvenience. It's my reputation. In all my twenty years at the bank, I've never been so much as a ha'penny out. I shall never face the chief cashier again.

AGATHA. Of course you will. You mustn't get upset. We all 'ave our little troubles.

MALLET. I've been saving for this day—saving as hard as I could. I've planned it all. And now look at me—lost. (*To* DORA.) You haven't seen anyone from Progressive?

DORA. Well, I wouldn't know them if I saw them, would I? You'd better ask the proprietor. He could tell you. (*Leading him to the archway.*)

MALLET. Yes, yes—I'd better do that.

DORA. The office is just through there on the right.

MALLET. Thank you. Thank you. Excuse me, won't you? (*He turns in the doorway.*) Oh, by the way, my name's Mallet. J. C. Mallet. Silly name, isn't it? Isn't it silly? (*Exit* MR. MALLET.)

DORA. Poor little chap. (*Goes to put magazine back* U.C.)

AGATHA. Ought to be taken about on a chain. Like a few other people I could mention. Feel better for your tea, then, Fiona?

FIONA. Oh, yes, it was quite nice, really.

AGATHA. You want to be careful. You nearly broke into a smile then. (*Goes to the french windows.*) Well, this *is* a nice little spot, isn't it?

DORA (*follows to* R. *of* AGATHA). It's lovely down there on the beach. I've never seen such sand. And the sea! They go water ski-ing, you know—just like on the pictures! You'd better try it.

AGATHA. I think I'm a bit on the 'eavy side for that sort of thing, dear. We might persuade Fiona to 'ave a go.

FIONA. I'm not doing anything dangerous.

AGATHA. Just a little joke. Do you go water ski-ing, Dora?

DORA. Oh, yea. I'm quite good at it, really. I expect that's because of my job. You soon get a sense of balance on the buses.

AGATHA. Oh, you're a bus conductress?

DORA. Yes.

FIONA. She doesn't look like one.

AGATHA. Oh, blimey, you don't expect her to come out 'ere in her uniform, do you? Do you like your job, dear?

DORA. It's all right. You get tired, though. I must walk miles in a day. Of course, you do meet some funny people during your day's work.

FIONA. If you come to work on our route you'll meet a few more. (*With a glance at* AGATHA.)

AGATHA. Oh? Getting bold, aren't we? I reckon the sun's gone to your 'ead already.

DORA. The other day a chap asked for Oldham. I told him we didn't go there and he got quite cross and said, "Well, it says so on the front." I soon put him in his place, though. I said, "It says Nestle's Milk on the back, but it doesn't mean to say we've been to Switzerland."

AGATHA. Do you all go down on the beach together, then? You know, in a sort of party.

DORA. Oh, no.

AGATHA. Why not?

DORA. Everyone keeps very much to themselves.

AGATHA. Well, I never! We'll soon see about that. I expect they want jollying up a bit! Just needs someone to break the ice, that's all. You just wait till the morning!

(HUBBACK *and his wife return from the archway. He is now wearing a panama hat and she has sun-glasses. They come to* U.C.)

All ready for your little stroll, then, General?

HUBBACK. Brigadier.

AGATHA. Oh, yes.

HUBBACK. Just as far as the newspaper kiosk and back. It's no more than a mashie shot away. See what's happening in dear old England.

AGATHA. That's right. (*Crossing below them to* FIONA.) You finished your tea, Fiona?

FIONA. Yes, Agatha.

AGATHA. Come on, then. We'd best go and unpack.

FIONA. Yes, Agatha. (*Moves* U.S. *and starts to collect the carrier bag, parcel, etc.*)

AGATHA (*to* R. *of the* HUBBACKS). I was just saying to Dora 'ere, won't it be fun all getting to know each other? We must organize lots of games and things on the beach tomorrow.

(BRIGADIER *and* MRS. HUBBACK *are shattered into silence.*)

Come along, then, Fiona. And do try and cheer up.

(AGATHA *and* FIONA *go off upstairs.*)

HUBBACK. She's a—a bright sort of person, isn't she?

DORA. I like her. I think she's going to be rather fun. Just what we need around here.

MRS. H. What do you mean by that?

DORA. Nothing. I was just thinking. I'm going on to the beach. 'bye!

(*Exit* DORA *by the french windows.* HUBBACK *eases* L., *watching her go.*)

MRS. H. (*aghast*). Did you hear what she said?

HUBBACK. She said she was going on to the beach.

MRS. H. Not her—the other one.

HUBBACK. Oh.

MRS. H. (*distastefully*). Beach games! (*Moves down to* C.)

HUBBACK. I don't expect she really meant it.

MRS. H. I knew something like this would happen. I said we should have gone to the South of France as usual.

HUBBACK. I don't think it's as bad as all that.

MRS. H. Don't you? Sometimes, Charles, I envy you your tolerance.

HUBBACK (*to* L. *of* MRS. H.). We can always go along to that other bit of beach. She can't find us there.

MRS. H. Can't she? I tell you, Charles, there'll be no more peace. That woman is liable to creep up on us, beaming all over her face, at any time from now on. Something will have to be done.

HUBBACK. Will it?

(*She turns to him suddenly.*)

MRS. H. You'll have to do something about it.

HUBBACK. Will I? Yes, of course—rather! I'll think of something, don't you worry. Let's go and get the paper.

MRS. H. All right. But do try to think of something other than the cricket scores!

> (*They are making for the archway as* MR. MALLET *wanders in, still in a cloud of depression.*)

MALLET. Excuse me. Are you Progressive Tours? Please say yes.

HUBBACK ⎫
MRS. H.   ⎬ (*together*). No!

MALLET. But you must help me. I'm lost.

HUBBACK. So are we—completely!

> (HUBBACK *and his wife go out by the archway.*)

MALLET (*brightening*). Oh, good! Then I'm not the only one! (*And he happily follows them off.*)

> (*A car is heard drawing up as* MALLET *disappears, followed by angry voices, one English, one Italian.*
>
> *After a moment* LEN BARRETT *appears at the open doorway, calling to someone outside. He is a brash, effervescent young cockney with a good deal of charm. He carries a suitcase and a grip.*)

LEN. You think yourself lucky, mate! Blimey, after a drive like that you ought to pay me!

> (*A torrent of angry Italian from outside.*)

Yes, and the same to you!

> (*He moves down into the room and is putting down his cases* U.C. *by the corner seat as* MARISA *comes down the stairs to his* R.)

MARISA. Buon giorno, signor.

LEN. Oh, don't say you don't speak English either. (*Sees her and melts.*) You don't need to speak anything.

MARISA. Good afternoon.

LEN. Yes—it is now.

MARISA. You are just arriving?

LEN. I didn't think I was going to the way that bloke was driving. Talk about Brands Hatch.

MARISA. You did not come on the coach with the others?

LEN. Not likely! There was a noisy old bag leading off at everyone. Oh, can she rabbit! I didn't fancy listening to her all the way, so I thought I'd take a taxi and have a butcher's at the scenery.

MARISA. Did you enjoy the scenery?

LEN. Enjoy it? I didn't see it. He didn't even slow down to go round the bends! And all the time talking fifteen to the dozen and looking over his shoulder at me! I said to him, "Mate", I said, "you keep your eyes on the bloomin' road. I want to get there, y'know!"

MARISA (*laughing*). You will get used to that.

LEN. You mean they all drive like that over 'ere?

MARISA. Most of the time.

LEN. Blimey, if Mrs. Castle could only see them!

MARISA. I will see which room you are in. What is your name, please?

LEN. Barrett. You can call me Len. (*As she starts to go.*) What's your name?

MARISA. Marisa.

LEN. Marisa, eh? Oh, that's nice. You know, sort of foreign. Yes, I like that.

> (*As* MARISA *goes out he emits a low wolf-whistle, and turns to see* DORA *coming in from the beach.*)

Blimey! The place is full of birds!

DORA. I forgot my sun oil.

LEN. You don't look like you need it. You're brown enough now.

DORA. I don't want to peel, though. I want to show it off when I get back home. You just arriving?

LEN. Yes. That's right.

DORA. It's very nice here.

LEN. Well, I like the look of what I've seen so far. (*Looks towards the archway where* MARISA *has gone off.*)

DORA. My name's Dora Cowley.

LEN. I'm Len Barrett. Here—whereabouts do you come from?

DORA. Lancashire.

LEN. Oh, that's it! I thought you was talking funny.

> (MARISA *comes in.*)

MARISA. You are in Room 25, Signor Barrett. You will follow me, please?

LEN. Ooh! You just give me half a chance! (*As she starts to pick up his suitcase.*) No, no! I'll take that. It's too 'eavy for a pretty girl like you. You take this one. (*Hands a small grip.*) Right—where are the apples and pears?

> (MARISA *on to the rostrum at the foot of the stairs as* FIONA *comes downstairs. She has her handbag and a travel brochure.* LEN *stands back to let her come past.*)

After you, your ladyship.

FIONA. Thank you, dear.

LEN. 'ere—haven't I seen you somewhere before?

FIONA. I've only just arrived.

LEN(*fearfully*). Did you come by train?

FIONA. Yes, that's right.

LEN. And—er—have you got a friend with you?

FIONA. She's not my friend. She's my sister. Perhaps you were on the same train, dear?

LEN. Yes, I'm afraid I was. I mean, I think I was. Oh. This is all I need!

(LEN *and* MARISA *go off upstairs.*)

FIONA (*moving to* C.). Funny chap. I wonder what's the matter with him.

DORA. Your room all right?

FIONA (*without enthusiasm*). Yes, it's quite nice really. Not like the Metropole, of course, but you can't 'ave everything, I suppose. (*Sits chair* L. *of table* L.C.)

DORA (*to* R. *of table* L.C.). You got a private bathroom?

FIONA. Yes. But it's ever so funny. Not like a proper bath at all. It's so small! I expect they found there wasn't room for a long one. But I shall feel so soppy sitting up in that thing.

DORA. You'll soon get used to it, Mrs. Francis.

FIONA. Miss Francis, dear.

DORA. Sorry. I thought perhaps you'd been married.

FIONA. Oh, no. I took one look at what 'appened to my sister and I said, "No. Not for me." (*Cheerfully*.) I'm a spinster, dear.

DORA (*glumly sitting* R. *of table* L.C.). So am I. Sounds awful, doesn't it? I do think they could have found a better word.

FIONA. Oh, I rather like it. Or perhaps I've just got used to it.

(*There is a short pause as they both give this a little thought. Then* DORA *snaps out of it.*)

DORA (*rising*). I'd better go and get my sun oil.

FIONA. Yes, I should, dear. You don't want to burn.

(DORA *goes off upstairs as* AGATHA *bustles on with some picture postcards.*)

AGATHA. Right! Here we are!

FIONA. What are these?

AGATHA. Picture postcards, of course. You got your pen?

FIONA. Yes, but—

AGATHA. Right—get on with them! (*Thrusts some of the cards at her.*)

FIONA. I don't see why we 'ave to write postcards now—

AGATHA. Well, we're 'ere, aren't we?

FIONA. Yes.

AGATHA. Right! Tell 'em we're 'ere! (*Sits* R. *of table* L.C.)

FIONA. Couldn't we do them tomorrow?

AGATHA. You'll forget 'em tomorrow. Do it now, then they're out of the way.

(*They start to write the postcards in silence.*)

FIONA. I don't know what to put.

AGATHA. Tell 'em you're enjoying yourself.

FIONA. But I'm not.

AGATHA. Well, tell 'em you're not enjoying yourself!

(*Pause. They write.*)

(*Looking up.*) Who's that one to?

FIONA. Mrs. Wilkinson.

AGATHA. What 'ave you put?

FIONA. "Mrs. Wilkinson, 22 Ferndale Avenue—"

AGATHA. Not that side—the other side! What 'ave you put on the other side?

FIONA (*after looking*). The picture's on the other side.

AGATHA. I mean the other side of the back!

FIONA. Oh. Nothing. You tell me what to say, Agatha.

AGATHA. Well, put something like—"This is a beautiful place. Wish you were with us."

FIONA. But I don't.

AGATHA. That doesn't matter! She's not likely to catch the next train.

FIONA (*writing*). "This is a beautiful place." (*Looks at the picture.*) But this isn't 'ere, this is San Remo.

AGATHA. What about it?

FIONA. But I 'aven't been there.

AGATHA. You went through it.

FIONA (*amazed*). Did I?

AGATHA (*patiently*). On the coach.

FIONA. I never noticed. (*Turns card over and crosses out what she has written.*)

AGATHA. Now what are you doing?

FIONA. I'm crossing out what I've written.

AGATHA. What for?

FIONA. Well, if I didn't notice it, how do I know it's a beautiful place?

AGATHA. For 'eaven's sake, it doesn't matter whether you noticed or not! She's not going to check up.

FIONA. Oh, I don't think I could do that.

AGATHA. Well, you think of something, then.

(DORA *comes in with sun oil. She puts one leg up on the corner seat and applies the oil.*)

DORA. You writing postcards already?

AGATHA. Like to get 'em off early.

DORA. I suppose I ought to send some. I've left it a bit late, though. If I send them now I'll be home almost as soon.

AGATHA. That doesn't matter, dear. Send them. Let them know you've been. (*To* FIONA.) How are you getting on?

FIONA (*writing laboriously*). All right.

AGATHA. You're not writing a novel, you know. I'd better send one to that Mrs. Fenwick.

FIONA. But you don't like her.

AGATHA. I don't care. I want to pay her back for the card she sent me from the South of France. (*Shows the card to* DORA.) What do you think of that one?

DORA. It's lovely. All those bright colours.

AGATHA (*with relish*). Yes. That'll show 'er! (*To* FIONA.) 'aven't you finished yet?

FIONA. Almost. (*She concludes by writing around the side of the card.*)

AGATHA. Well, what 'ave you put?

FIONA (*reading*). "We are three minutes from the gently sloping beach of honey-coloured sand—"

AGATHA. What?

FIONA. "—and the warm caressing Mediterranean sea. Behind us the hillside villas gleam white and fresh amongst the pencil-like cypress trees and colour-drunk flowers."

AGATHA. The what?

FIONA (*looking up*). Colour-drunk flowers.

AGATHA. I see. Go on.

FIONA. "The air is warm and 'eavy with scent, and we are enjoying these enchanted shores."

AGATHA. 'ere! You don't want to overdo it, you know. 'ow did you think all that up?

FIONA. It's all 'ere in the brotcher. (*Waves brochure at* AGATHA.)

AGATHA. You can't put that.

FIONA. Why not? What 'ave you put?

AGATHA (*reading*). "Spending a fortnight 'ere on the Italian Riveera. It's very nice and very expensive. I bet you wish you were here." There! That's to the point, isn't it?

DORA. Yes. I don't think she's liable to misunderstand that.

(JULIAN WHITTLE *comes in from the main entrance. He is about 35, and of a serious disposition. He is English and intelligent in appearance, and wears linen trousers and a dull shirt. He is rather hot and is mopping his brow as he enters. He comes to* C.)

WHITTLE. Good afternoon, everyone.

DORA. Hullo, Mr. Whittle. You do look hot.

WHITTLE. I feel hot. The walk up that hill from the main road really is dreadful. I can't think why they had to build up as far as this.

DORA. Well, it's such a lovely view.

WHITTLE (*unimpressed*). Oh. Yes, I suppose it was that. (*To* AGATHA.) I'm awfully sorry I wasn't there to meet you off the coach, but you know how it is—pressure of work. And this beastly climate doesn't make for agility of action. I would have been there—I meant to be there—

AGATHA. But you weren't there.

WHITTLE (*a little put out*). Er—precisely. I really am sorry.

AGATHA. That's all right. We weren't expecting you anyway.

WHITTLE (*with a watery smile*). It's kind of you to say so, but I think you were.

AGATHA. I think I should know if I was expecting you or not.

WHITTLE. But my name's Whittle.

AGATHA. You ever 'eard of Mr. Whittle, Fiona?

FIONA. I don't think so.

AGATHA. No, Mr. Whittle, you weren't expected.

WHITTLE. I'm terribly sorry. I must have mistaken you for someone else. (*Sits exhausted* R. *of table* R.C. *and mops his brow.*)

(MARISA *and* LEN *come in from the archway.*)

MARISA (*to* LEN). I hope you find everything all right, Signor Barrett.

LEN (*eyeing her*). Everything looks all right to me.

FIONA. Agatha, this young man was on the same train as us. Young man—(*He is intent on* MARISA.) Young man!

LEN (*coming to*). Yes?

FIONA. This is my sister.

LEN. Oh, blimey, so it is!

AGATHA. What took you so long getting here then? Didn't you know about the coach?

LEN. Well—er—yes, I did—yes.

AGATHA. Well, I do think they might 'ave waited for you.

LEN. As a matter of fact, I preferred to come on my own. (*He escapes to the french windows and looks out.*)

AGATHA. Really? You should 'ave come with us. We 'ad a lovely sing-song, didn't we, Fiona?

FIONA. Yes, Agatha, lovely.

(WHITTLE *speaks to* MARISA, *who is on her way to the door* D.R.)

WHITTLE. Marisa, I've come all this way on a wild-goose chase and now I'm exhausted. How about one of those long orange and sodas?

MARISA (D.R.). I will get it.

WHITTLE. I was supposed to meet two old bags off the afternoon coach, but they seem to have got mislaid. I suppose there's no message about a—(*Consulting some papers.*)—a Mrs. Hepworth and a Miss Francis?

MARISA. But they are here.

WHITTLE. Where?

MARISA. Over there. (*Indicates* AGATHA *and* FIONA.)

WHITTLE. Oh, my God! (*Sinks his face into his hands.*)

AGATHA (*rising to her full height*). I am Mrs. Hepworth, Mr. Whittle! And the other old bag is my sister Fiona!

WHITTLE (*rising to below table* R.C.). I'm awfully sorry. But you said you weren't expecting me,

AGATHA. As far as I am concerned we're not.

WHITTLE. But if you are Mrs. Hepworth and this is your sister, you must be. (*To* MARISA.) I'll have a little gin with that orange.

(MARISA *goes off* D.R.)

(*In to* D.C.) You are with Eagle, aren't you?

AGATHA. Yes.

WHITTLE. Well, I'm your Eagle representative.

AGATHA. Oh, no you're not!

WHITTLE. But I assure you!

AGATHA. Oh, no!

WHITTLE. But I am! I've been here since the end of May.

AGATHA. I can't 'elp that!

WHITTLE (*very patiently*). Mrs. Hepworth, I promise you—

AGATHA. I don't want none of your promises! It's all down 'ere in the brotcher—if we 'ave any queries, etc. we 'ave to go to "Julian". He's our Eagle representative and he'll deal with us. That right, Fiona?

FIONA. Yes, Agatha, that's the one for us—"Julian".

WHITTLE. Well—I am "Julian".

AGATHA. You said your name was Whittle.

WHITTLE. It is. The company prefer to call us by our Christian names alone. They seem to think it gives an air of bonhomie to the proceedings.

AGATHA. Well, you 'aven't started off very well, 'ave you, Mr. Whittle?

FIONA. "Julian", Agatha.

AGATHA. He's Mr. Whittle to me! (*Sits again and turns her back on* WHITTLE.)

WHITTLE (*trying hard, moving to* R. *of* AGATHA). If you have any worries, queries, problems—come to me. (*To above table.*) I'm to be found every day between eleven and twelve at the Cafe Romana, and every evening from six to seven I'm in the bar of the Marini. (*Above* FIONA *to* L. *of table.*) There are certain fascinating trips from day to day to various beauty spots and places of historic interest. You can book all these through me. There's a trip to the mountains in a rather nasty little coach which is quite fun in a rather macabre way, and a wine tasting on Tuesdays and Fridays which I can thoroughly recommend.

(*Below the table to* D.C.) I'll be popping in and out, so don't hesitate to stop me and ask anything you like. (*To* MARISA *as she enters with his drink.*) Is that my gin?

MARISA. *Si, signor.*

WHITTLE. Thank you. (*Sits* R. *of table* R.C. *and drinks deeply.*)

DORA (*moving towards the french windows*). Well, I'm going down to the beach now. I don't suppose anybody wants to be shown the way, do they? (*Ends up looking hopefully at* LEN.)

LEN (*escaping to* D.L.). Well, I thought I'd have a cup of tea first.

DORA. All right. I expect I'll see you all later. Ta-ra.

AGATHA. I expect we'll be down there in the morning, Dora.

DORA (*a little doubtful at this prospect*). Oh. Oh, yes. That'll be lovely.

(*Exit* DORA *to the beach.*)

AGATHA. She's a sweet girl, isn't she?

MARISA. Shall I get you some tea, then, Mr. Barrett?

LEN. Tea? No fear!

MARISA. But you said—

LEN. Oh! Oh, yes—well, I don't think I will after all. I think I'll have one of those orange drinks. They look okay.

MARISA. *Si, signor.* (*Exit* MARISA D.R.)

WHITTLE. I can thoroughly recommend it for this beastly weather.

LEN (*below table* L.C. *to* D.C.). Don't you like the heat?

WHITTLE. No fear. I keep in the shade as much as I can.

LEN. How long have you been out here?

WHITTLE. Since May. I stay until the end of September.

LEN (*to above table* R.C.). Nice job!

WHITTLE. That's what I thought. But take my word for it, it isn't.

LEN. Why not? Good food, beautiful sea, the sun shining, and plenty of birds. What's wrong with that?

WHITTLE. My dear fellow, can you imagine looking after a lot of old— (*Checks himself as he remembers* AGATHA.)—looking after a lot of English trippers all set to "have themselves a ball"?

LEN. Then how did you come to take on the job?

WHITTLE. I spoke Italian, and suddenly got tired of selling insurance. I thought a change of air would do me good.

LEN. It will. By the end of September you'll have a sun-tan like a native.

WHITTLE. I'm afraid not.

LEN. Why?

WHITTLE. I peel. Two minutes in this sort of heat and I turn pink like a piece of litmus paper. That's why whenever I can I hurry for the shade.

AGATHA. It was strange I didn't recognize you from your picture in the brotcher, Mr. Whittle.

WHITTLE. It was taken a long time ago. I've aged and soured since then.

FIONA. All this foreign travel's overrated, I say.

AGATHA. How do you know? You've only been 'ere five minutes. You might go down on the beach one day and become a new woman. You might sit down there on the pie-arsa.

LEN. On the what?

WHITTLE. I think she means *piazza*.

AGATHA. That's it! You might sit there and meet Mr. Right.

FIONA. Mr. Right?

AGATHA. Your dream man!

FIONA. Well, if he turns out like your Harold, it won't arf be a nightmare. (*She enjoys this at* AGATHA's *expense*.)

    (MARISA *comes in with orange drink, and puts it down in front of* LEN.)

LEN. Oh, thanks. (*Gazing at her.*) Very nice.

    (*She squirts the soda into his drink and he reacts.*)

    Oh, ta!

              (*Exit* MARISA D.R.)

FIONA (*to* LEN). Is your wife with you, dear?

LEN (*appalled at the suggestion*). Blimey! I'm not married. (*He retires with his drink to the corner seat* U.C.)

FIONA. Fancy free, eh? Same as me! I never went in for that sort of thing, you know. Do you like coming out here on your own, young man?

LEN. Yes, why not?

FIONA. You are a funny one.

AGATHA. Well, we shall see you aren't lonely—won't we, Fiona? Nothing like plenty of good friends around, that's what I always say!

WHITTLE. Perhaps Mr. Barrett wants to be alone.

AGATHA. Wants to be alone? Oh, no! He may think he does, but he doesn't really. Do you?

LEN. Well, I—

AGATHA. No, of course not! Get you down there on the beach throwing a ball about and you'll soon forget all about being alone.

    (BRIGADIER *and* MRS. HUBBACK *come in by the french windows. He is carrying the newspapers.*)

    Ah! there you are, Major!

HUBBACK. Er—Brigadier.

AGATHA. Yes—sorry—I keep forgetting. You were a long time.

HUBBACK. Yes. Bit of a queue for the newspapers.

MRS. H. (*to armchair* D.L. *to sit*). Some people would queue for anything. You'd think war had been declared to see the anxious faces jockeying for position.

HUBBACK. Only natural, m'dear. Miles away. Foreign land and all that. Like to know what's going on in the old country.

WHITTLE. And what is going on?

HUBBACK (*above* AGATHA *to* C.). Pretty grim, I'm afraid. Five wickets down. Only fifty runs on the board.

MRS. H. Ridiculous game. You men are like a lot of children.

HUBBACK. More of your brood arriving today?

WHITTLE. They have arrived.

HUBBACK (*turning to* AGATHA). Oh! Are you with Whittle?

AGATHA. Yes, we are. (*Coldly.*) Mr. Whittle has just introduced himself.

FIONA. Doesn't look a bit like his photo.

WHITTLE. Still, you had an advantage over me. You at least knew what I was going to be like.

HUBBACK. Has Mr. Whittle told you about the various trips at your disposal?

AGATHA. Yes, he 'as.

HUBBACK. I can recommend them all!

AGATHA. We didn't come 'ere to go on trips, you know.

HUBBACK. Oh, but you must! I mean, there are so many fascinating things to see. Aren't there, Whittle?

WHITTLE. Yes, rather.

HUBBACK. You wouldn't want to come all the way out here and go back having not seen the sights, would you? Be like going to Blackpool and not seeing the Tower. Wouldn't it, Whittle?

WHITTLE. A very apt simile, sir.

HUBBACK. Mr. Whittle could arrange a trip for you every day. Couldn't you, Whittle?

WHITTLE. With pleasure.

FIONA. If we go on a trip every day we'll never be 'ere!

HUBBACK (*with feigned surprise*). No. No, you wouldn't, would you? (*Glances desperately at* WHITTLE.)

FIONA. But we've come 'ere, Agatha.

AGATHA. 'course we 'ave—(*Rising to her full height.*)—and we're not moving. Mr. Whittle can arrange as many trips as he likes! I reckon we can 'ave just as much fun 'ere, don't you, Fiona?

FIONA. Well, Agatha—

AGATHA. Of course we can! Lots of games on the beach—and I expect there'll be music and dancing at night. We'll all 'ave a lovely time!

And as me and Fiona 'aven't been 'ere before we'll need someone who knows their way around. That's where you come in, Colonel.

HUBBACK. Brigadier.

AGATHA (*elbowing him slyly*). I bet you know where to find plenty of night life, don't you? You can show us the town. And if Mr. Whittle behaves 'imself he can come, too! (*Below table* L.C. *to collect* FIONA.) Oh, I can't wait to get started! Come along, Fiona! We 'aven't even 'ad a look at the village yet.

FIONA. I don't think I want to—

AGATHA (*on* L. *of* FIONA). Don't be silly, of course you do!

FIONA. I'm tired.

AGATHA. Tired of sitting down, that's what you're tired of! Bit of exercise do you the world of good. Come on! (*Pulls* FIONA *to her feet and drags her towards the french windows.*)

FIONA. It won't be like seeing the shops at Eastcliffe—

AGATHA. Well, you can't expect to find your Boots and your Marks and Spencers!

FIONA. Oh, dear—

AGATHA. But they'll 'ave something similar! Come on, now. Good-bye, everybody! We shan't be long. Toodle-oo!

FIONA (*grumbling*, D.L. *of* AGATHA). If I was at Eastcliffe—

AGATHA. Fiona Francis, I'm telling you for positively the last time—I don't want to 'ear no more about Eastcliffe. You understand? I'm sick of the sound of it. And I'm sick of you going about with a long face. You remember this, Fiona Francis—you came out 'ere to enjoy yourself,—and I'm going to see that you do!

(AGATHA *propels* FIONA *off through the french windows, leaving the others standing gazing speechlessly after them.*)

CURTAIN

ACT TWO

SCENE I

The following morning. The sun is shining brightly. MARISA, *with a tray, is collecting some dirty cups and saucers from the table* R.C. LEN *comes in from the beach entrance. He is wearing linen slacks and a gay shirt.*

LEN. Good morning, Marisa!

MARISA. *Buon giorno, signor.* I did not know that you were up.

LEN. You ever tried to sleep with a cement mixer going under your window? When I booked this 'oliday nobody said nothing about them building next door to the hotel!

MARISA. That is the new annexe.

LEN. Oh, is it? These blokes start early enough, don't they? If they did that in England we'd all go on strike! I couldn't get much kip once they'd started up, so I went for a little stroll. You know, down the old beach. Very nice. Here, I'm not too late for breakfast, am I?

MARISA. Oh, no. It is served until ten o'clock.

LEN. Good.

(*She starts to move towards table* L.C., *but he gets in her way.*)

Where's the best place to swim, then, Marisa? You know—somewhere quiet.

MARISA. Along to the right. Not many people go there because you have to dive in off the rocks.

(*She starts to move and he intercepts her again.*)

LEN. Is that where you go?

MARISA. Sometimes. (*Patiently.*) Signor Barrett—I have work to do.

(*She passes him and goes to table* L.C. *to collect dirty cup and saucer.*)

LEN (*following her*). Are you a good swimmer, Marisa?

MARISA. Out here children can swim almost as soon as they can walk.

LEN. Do you get much time to go on the beach yourself?

MARISA. Sometimes I go in the afternoon.

LEN (*hopefully*). On your own?

MARISA. No. I have four brothers. They are very big and very strong.

LEN. Oh, are they!

(*She passes below him towards door* D.R. *as* DORA *enters from the stairs. She is wearing a sun-dress.*)

DORA. Good morning.

LEN. Oh, hullo.

DORA. I didn't see you at breakfast.

LEN. Haven't had any yet.

DORA. There weren't many people down for breakfast this morning. It was ever so empty.

MARISA. Today more people have had breakfast in their rooms.

DORA. Would you have some coffee sent up to Rene, please?

MARISA. She is no better today?

DORA. Afraid not.

MARISA. Perhaps a croissant and butter?

DORA. I don't think so. One look would set her right off.

MARISA. Very well. Excuse me, please.

LEN. I'll be in for breakfast in a couple of minutes, Marisa.

(*Exit* MARISA D.R.)

DORA (*coming downstage to* C., *coyly*). I wonder what you two were talking about when I came in.

LEN (*he relaxes, man-of-the-world, in chair* R. *of table* R.C.). You wouldn't half be surprised!

DORA. You know what these Continentals are—hot-blooded! I should think she goes after every man she sees.

LEN. I can't help it if she takes a shine to me.

DORA (*to above table* L.C.). How long are you staying?

LEN. Ten days.

DORA. You're lucky. We go back on Friday, me and Rene.

LEN. Oh, she's your friend?

DORA. Yes. The first day here she took one mouthful and off she went like greasy lightning. Been in her room ever since.

LEN. You haven't much time left, then, if you go back on Friday?

DORA (*pathetically*). No.

(MARISA *comes in* D.R. *with flowers in a vase and a duster.*)

MARISA (*to* DORA). I have sent up coffee to your friend.

DORA. Oh, thanks.

LEN (*crossing beaming to* MARISA). Well now, you gorgeous thing, perhaps you'd like to come and serve mine for me, eh?

MARISA (*coldly*). It is already served, Signor Barrett. (*She moves above him to put flowers on table* U.C. DORA *giggles.*)

LEN. Oh. All right. (*He goes* D.R., *slightly crestfallen.*)

(HUBBACK *appears at the archway, peers in cautiously, then turns and speaks offstage to his wife.*)

HUBBACK. All right, m'dear. All clear!

(HUBBACK *and his wife enter to* U.R.C. *She has a book; he carries a camera and his panama.*)

DORA (*R. of chair* R. *of table* L.C.). Hullo, Brigadier.

HUBBACK. Ah, hullo there! Morning, Marisa.

MARISA. *Buon giorno.* (*To* MRS. H.) *Buon giorno, signora.*

MRS. H. Good morning, Marisa.

DORA. You coming on the beach this morning, Brigadier?

HUBBACK. Very likely, m'dear. Very likely.

> (MRS. H. *gives him a look of patient forbearance.*)

Any sign of Mrs. Hepworth and her sister, Marisa?

MARISA. Miss Francis is finishing her breakfast. Mrs. Hepworth has gone down to the village.

HUBBACK. Good.

MARISA. She will not be long. (*Busies herself tidying magazines, dusting, etc.*)

HUBBACK. Not so good.

DORA. Didn't see you at breakfast this morning, Brigadier.

HUBBACK. No. We decided we'd have it up in our room.

DORA. Mrs. Hepworth was asking where you were.

HUBBACK. Oh, was she? Thought we'd got out on to the beach. If we don't get out of the way early, she'll have us all building sand castles before you can say Jack Robinson.

DORA. That's why there were so few people in the dining-room for breakfast?

HUBBACK. I should think most people have scuttled away and hidden themselves by now.

DORA. It seems a bit unkind, doesn't it?

HUBBACK. Unkind? You saw the way she carried on at dinner last night. Actually calling out across the room to everyone. I've never been so humiliated. People will soon begin to think that I'm not a Brigadier at all! Well, come on, m'dear. Better go and find a bit of cover before Mrs. Hepworth spots us.

> (*They are about to go as* AGATHA *comes pounding in through the main door. She is dressed in a lurid floral dress, sandals, dark glasses and a straw hat. She is rosy and beaming. She carries a beach bag and another straw hat.*)

AGATHA. Aaah! Caught you just in time! *Buon giorno,* everyone! (*Moves* D.C. *and places her beach bag on the chair* L. *of table* R.C.)

HUBBACK (*deflated*). Good morning, Mrs. Hepworth.

AGATHA. You just going off to the beach, Dora?

DORA. Yes, I was—

AGATHA. Well, don't. You wait just a minute.

DORA (L. *of table* L.C.). Well, I thought—

AGATHA (*to* R. *of* HUBBACK). Now, general—

HUBBACK. Brigadier!

AGATHA. There I go again! (*Playfully.*) Now, what happened to us at breakfast this morning? We weren't on parade, were we?

HUBBACK. Well, no—actually my wife felt a little—peculiar—

AGATHA. Yes, I can see she doesn't look too good. (*To* MRS. H.) We'll get you chasing a ball about the beach. That'll soon put the roses back.

MRS. H. I thought actually a little stroll into the village—

AGATHA (*with finality*). You're too late. I've just been. What do you think of this hat? Suits me, don't you think? Keeps the sun off a treat.

HUBBACK. I thought the idea was to get the sun on.

AGATHA. You can't overdo it, you know. You got to be careful. Any sign of that sister of mine, Marisa?

MARISA (*down on* R. *of* AGATHA). I think she has gone back up to her room.

AGATHA. And a good thing, too. Gone to change, I expect. You should 'ave seen her at breakfast. Hot morning like this and she comes down in a tweed skirt and a jumper! I said to her, "Fiona", I said, "the minute you finish your breakfast, upstairs you go and change," I said. "You can't go on the beach like that," I said. "What will people think?" I mean, I don't want people pointing at us and having a laugh at our expense. I said to her, I said, "The least you can do is put on a cotton print." I've brought this other hat for 'er, too. Thought she'd need it. She's not used to the sun, y'know. Got a very soft skin. Couple of minutes out in this 'eat and she'd look like a cinder! Be a dear, Marisa love, and pop up and tell 'er to 'urry.

MARISA. Si, signora. (*She goes upstairs.*)

AGATHA (*to above the table, examining the contents of her bag*). We mustn't keep you all waiting, must we? Bet you're dying to get on to the beach.

HUBBACK (*coming forward tentatively*). Well, actually, we were thinking of popping into the village. Few things I want to buy.

AGATHA (*ominously*). Oh?

HUBBACK. You know, shaving-cream, things like that.

AGATHA. That's all right. Here you are. (*She produces a tube of shaving cream from her bag.*) I 'eard you mention last night that you needed some, so I thought I'd save you the trouble.

HUBBACK. That's—that's very kind of you.

AGATHA. Think nothing of it. Saved you the journey.

HUBBACK. Well, there was something else I needed.

AGATHA. What was that?

HUBBACK. Er—the morning paper.

AGATHA. It doesn't come out until the afternoon.

HUBBACK. No, of course not. I forgot.

AGATHA. So you don't need to go to the village at all, do you?

HUBBACK. Apparently not.

DORA. Well, if you'll excuse me, I think—

AGATHA. Where are you going, Dora?

DORA. To the beach.

AGATHA. Yes, dear, but just wait a minute—we're all coming. Where's that sister of mine? (*Goes off, calling.*) Fiona! What are you doing? (*Ad lib.*)

HUBBACK. Come on—quickly!

> (DORA, HUBBACK *and* MRS. HUBBACK *make a concerted move towards the french windows, but are caught in the act as* AGATHA *returns.*)

AGATHA (*crossing to them*). Now, now! You all trying to get there before us? Much better if we all go down together, or we might not find you on the beach, and that would never do, would it? (*Taking* MRS. HUBBACK *to chair* D.L.) You better sit down till we're all ready, Mrs. 'ubback. Can't 'ave you standing about feeling the way you do. (*Forces* MRS. H. *to sit down.*) Oh, I almost forgot! (*She goes back to her beach bag.*)

HUBBACK. What?

> (AGATHA *takes something out of her bag.*)

AGATHA. 'ere you are. A beach ball! (*Hands him the beach ball.*)

HUBBACK. I don't want it.

AGATHA (*playfully*). Oh, yes, you do—we're Officer Commanding beach ball, now, that's what we are!

HUBBACK. We are nothing of the sort!

AGATHA. He is, isn't he, Dora?

DORA (*to above table* L.C., *giggling*). Yes, of course he is!

AGATHA. There you are—proposed and seconded. You'd better start blowing.

HUBBACK. What?

AGATHA. Well, you don't think we can kick it about on the beach like that, do you?

HUBBACK. But I've never blown up a thing like this in my life.

AGATHA. Then it's 'igh time you started.

HUBBACK. I refuse—absolutely!

DORA. Oh, Brigadier, you are a spoilsport. You only 'ave to blow it up. That's not much for a big strong man like you, is it?

HUBBACK (*melting*). Well, I—

MRS. H. For heaven's sake blow it up and get it over.

HUBBACK. Very well, m'dear. (*He tries to blow it up, but has no success.*)

AGATHA. You 'aven't much wind, 'ave you?

HUBBACK. I told you, I'm not used to this sort of thing.

AGATHA. Keep trying.

(He tries again, but is again unsuccessful.)

HUBBACK. I can't do it.

DORA. Oh, dear.

HUBBACK. Well, I'm sorry.

AGATHA. Just fancy—Army man like you and you can't blow better than that.

HUBBACK. I was a Brigadier, not a bugler!

AGATHA. Well, never mind. I expect that young man will be able to do it. Where is he, by the way?

DORA. I think he's having his breakfast.

AGATHA. There's something strange about him, you know, I said so from the beginning. Ever since he said he didn't want to travel on the coach with the rest of us. I think there's more in him than meets the eve.

DORA. What does meet the eye seems quite nice. (*She giggles shyly.*)

AGATHA. Oh, I see, Dora! That's why you're so keen to sneak off to the beach before the rest of us? You be careful. I've 'eard of people like 'im before. White slavers! Put your sun-hat over your eyes for two minutes, and the next thing you know you're in Morocco.

DORA. He wouldn't be anything like that.

AGATHA. All right—you see. Only don't say I didn't warn you. Where's that sister of mine? (*To door.*) Fiona!

FIONA (*off*). Coming, Agatha!

AGATHA. About time, too. (*Returning to the others.*) She'd be late for her own funeral.

(Enter FIONA. She is dressed in a shapeless floral silk dress and white plimsolls.)

FIONA (*nervously*). Good morning, everyone.

ALL. Good morning.

AGATHA. Well, come on—let's 'ave a look at you.

(FIONA advances.)

Other side.

(FIONA turns round.)

Yes, you'll do. You kept us all waiting.

FIONA. Did I?

AGATHA. Yes. All these people want to go on the beach. We couldn't go until you arrived.

HUBBACK. Did you sleep well, Miss Francis?

FIONA. It took me a long time to get off. They're very noisy in the streets 'ere at night, aren't they? I suppose that's because they're Continental.

AGATHA. You slept well enough when it was time to get up this morning, I note. Nearly made us miss our breakfast.

FIONA. Funny sort of a breakfast, too, wasn't it? Just coffee and rolls. In England you get porridge or fruit juice with eggs and bacon to follow—

AGATHA. Well, you're in Italy now, Fiona, so for 'eaven's sake try to behave like a native! What's wrong with coffee and rolls for a change?

FIONA. And no proper marmalade.

AGATHA. What are you grumbling about? You brought your pot of Golden Shred, didn't you?

FIONA. I feel so guilty sneaking it into the dining-room in my 'andbag.

AGATHA. There's nothing wrong in that.

FIONA (downstage a little). I'm sorry if I kept you all waiting.

ALL. That's all right. Think nothing of it, etc. etc.

FIONA. You see, I 'ad to go and change.

AGATHA. I should think so, too. Coming down all muffled up as if it was the middle of winter.

DORA. Well, you look very nice now, Miss Francis.

FIONA (pleased). Do you like it?

DORA. Very pretty.

FIONA. I saw it advertised in a newspaper and I took a fancy to it right away, so I cut out the coupon and sent it up.

AGATHA. You got the camera?

FIONA. Oh, Agatha, I forgot!

AGATHA. Fiona Francis, you are the limit! I distinctly told you to go up and change and to make sure you bring the camera down with you. I do wish you'd try and improve. I don't ask you to do many things, 'eaven knows, but I wish you'd try to do them when I do!

FIONA. I'll go and get it now—

AGATHA. You'll do nothing of the sort. We don't want you going off again or we'll be 'ere all morning. (To door.) Marisa, dear! (To FIONA again.) We've waited long enough as it is.

FIONA. You could 'ave gone without me.

AGATHA. We'd 'ave never 'eard the end of it if we 'ad.

FIONA. I wouldn't 'ave minded. I'd like a quiet sit down. I 'aven't finished reading my Woman's Own yet.

AGATHA. You didn't come 'ere to read. You could 'ave stopped at 'ome to do that.

FIONA. Yes, and I wish I 'ad.

AGATHA (*as* MARISA *comes downstairs*). Ah, Marisa! Be a dear and slip up to my room and fetch the camera that's on the bed, will you?

MARISA. *Si, signora.*

(*Exit* MARISA.)

AGATHA (*to above table* R.C.). She is a sweet girl, isn't she? Always so 'appy and smiling. I like to see people 'appy and smiling—you listening, Fiona?—there's enough misery in the world. Don't you think so, Captain?

HUBBACK. Brigadier. Yes, indeed I do.

MRS. H. (*rising*). I should like to go on to the beach.

AGATHA. Yes, dear, and so you shall in a minute. (MRS. H. *sits again*.) 'ere you are, Fiona. This is for you. (*Hands* FIONA *the sun hat*.)

FIONA (*looking at it curiously*). What's it for?

AGATHA. You put it on your 'ead.

FIONA. I shall look so silly.

AGATHA. You're not going in for a Beauty Competition.

FIONA. But it's so big.

AGATHA. You'll only complain if you get out in the 'eat and get burned up. Get it on!

(FIONA *puts the hat on well over her eyes. Her face is completely hidden*.)

FIONA. I can't see.

AGATHA. You don't 'ave to wear it like a cowboy! (*Straightens the hat*.)

(MARISA *comes in with a small Brownie camera. She crosses to* R. *of* AGATHA.)

Thank you, love. That was kind.

MARISA. *Prego.*

AGATHA (*collects her beach bag and crosses below* FIONA *to* C.). I think we're all ready now, then, aren't we? As soon as we get down on the beach I want to take a nice snap of you all in a group. All right, Fiona, you ready now? (*Crosses to* MRS. H. *and pulls her to her feet*.) Come along Mrs. Hubback, I'm sorry to 'ave kept you waiting. (*Up to* L. *of* HUBBACK.) Now, Brigadier—there! I got it right that time, didn't I? Have you got the beach ball?

HUBBACK. No. You took it back.

AGATHA. Oh, yes, that young man was going to blow it up, wasn't he? He's taking a long time, isn't he? Well, I tell you what, Marisa. Tell him to follow us down as soon as he's ready. We'll watch out for him.

DORA. I'll wait for him if you like, Mrs. Hepworth.

AGATHA. Oh, no, Dora dear. I want you in front of the photo. Marisa will tell him. Come along, then everyone—off we go!

(*Everyone starts for the french windows, talking ad lib. as they go.*)
Fiona, for 'eaven's sake don't dawdle about!

(Fiona *is standing very still, rooted to the spot, turning slightly green.* Dora, Hubback, Mrs. H. *and* Agatha *are in a group by the french windows.*)

Now what's the matter?

Fiona. I don't feel very well.

Agatha. Oh, blimey!

Fiona. I think I'd better sit down for a minute. (*She does so in chair* L. *of table* R.C.).

(*They all come back a little from the french windows.* Agatha *to* U.L. *of* Fiona.)

Marisa. I will get you some water, Miss Francis. (*She goes* D.R.)

Hubback. Bad luck, The change of air, that's what it is. Sometimes affects you on the first day. Better sit still for a while. Keep out of the sun.

Dora. Just how it took my friend Rene! First day—down she went like a pack of cards!

Agatha. Don't encourage 'er, Dora! There's nothing wrong with 'er. A glass of water and she'll be as right as rain.

Hubback. All the same, better sit still for half an hour or so.

Fiona (*the voice of doom*). It's 'appening to me, Agatha.

Agatha. What's 'appening to you?

Fiona. The same as 'appened to that woman I told you about. Bit by a bug she was. Passed right away!

Agatha. You're not going to pass away. And besides you 'aven't been bitten by a bug.

Fiona. 'ow do I know, Agatha? 'ow can I be sure?

Agatha. Because you'd 'ave felt something.

Fiona. It might 'ave 'appened in the night! I said we should 'ave 'ad mosquito nets.

Agatha. You don't need mosquito nets 'ere! Oh, blimey, this is all I need!

Hubback. How about a spot of brandy?

Fiona (*brightening*). Oh, well, that would be nice—

Agatha (*firmly*). She doesn't drink.

Hubback. Oh. Well, if you'll excuse us we'll totter down to the beach. See you later, eh? Sorry you can't come with us. (*To* Mrs. H.) Come along, m'dear!

(Hubback, Mrs. H. *and* Dora *go out hurriedly by the french windows before* Agatha *can prevent them.*
Marisa *returns with a glass of water. She comes to above table* R.C.)

AGATHA (*taking it*). Thanks, love. That was good of you. (*Holding it to* FIONA.) 'ere you are, take some of this.

(FIONA *sips the water. There is a pause.*)

Feel better now?

FIONA. I went all peculiar.

AGATHA. You didn't 'ave far to go.

FIONA. Do you think I'm going to die, Agatha?

AGATHA. I shouldn't be surprised. You might at least 'ave waited till we got back 'ome.

MARISA. You are not going to die, Miss Francis.

FIONA. Aren't I?

MARISA. No, of course not. You will soon be all right, then you can go down on the beach. You will feel better in the fresh air.

FIONA. Thank you, dear. That is kind of you.

MARISA. I am through there if you want me.

(MARISA *goes by the archway. A pause.*)

AGATHA. I suppose you realize what you've done?

FIONA. No. What?

AGATHA. Made us both a laughing-stock, that's what. I've never been so ashamed. And now they've gone on without us. 'eaven knows if we'll find them down there on the beach.

FIONA. I couldn't 'elp it. I ate something that disagreed with me.

AGATHA. What, pray? This morning you 'ad rolls and butter and coffee, and last night you turned up your nose at every course on the menu. Now don't tell me that anyone—even you—can get ill on three omelettes.

FIONA. The eggs aren't like the ones in England.

AGATHA. Even out 'ere, Fiona, the eggs still come from the 'ens!

FIONA. I knew a woman once who died after eating eggs.

AGATHA. Yes, I'm sure you did.

FIONA. She went all purple and died.

AGATHA. Well, you're still white, so you've got a long way to go yet.

(LEN *comes in from the dining-room.*)

LEN (*to* U.R. *of chair* R. *of table* R.C.). I thought you'd be down on the beach.

AGATHA. We would 'ave been, but my sister 'as come over queer.

LEN. Anything I can do?

AGATHA. No. She's past 'ope, Mr. Barrett. (*Rising.*)

FIONA. I can't 'elp it if I'm ill. I think I'd better go up to my room and 'ave a lay down.

AGATHA. Yes, I should if I were you. If you're going to pass out you may as well do it in comfort.

FIONA. And I'll take one of these pills.

AGATHA. They're for travel sickness.

FIONA. Maybe that's what I've got.

AGATHA. But you've only walked down the stairs. You can't call that travelling!

FIONA. Perhaps it's delayed action. I'm paying now for yesterday.

AGATHA (*to* LEN). What can you do with 'er? I ask you, what can you do with 'er?

> (FIONA *makes for the archway.*)

'ere, wait a minute. I'd better come with you to see you're all right.

FIONA (*the Christian martyr*). No! No, Agatha, I don't want to be a trouble to anyone. If I'm going to die, I'll die on my own. (*Exit* FIONA.)

AGATHA. She'll drive me out of my mind one of these days. She didn't want to come 'ere, you see, and this is her way of paying me back. We were all going on the beach together until this 'appened. I hope they'll keep an eye out for us. (*To french windows.*)

LEN. I bet they will!

AGATHA. You going to join them?

> (MARISA *comes in from the archway.*)

LEN (*eyeing* MARISA). Well, I—I thought I'd stick around the hotel this morning.

MARISA. Is your sister any better, Mrs. Hepworth?

AGATHA. She's gone to 'ave a little lay down.

MARISA. It will be a pity if she misses her first day on the beach. (*To* LEN, *who is gazing at her enraptured.*) Why do you not go on to the beach, Signor Barrett?

LEN. I thought I'd stay 'ere and talk to you.

MARISA. I have work to do.

LEN. You could take a few minutes off.

> (DORA *comes in from the french windows.*)

DORA. I forgot my bag!

AGATHA. It's on your arm, dear.

DORA. Oh. Oh, yes. So it is. (*Crosses* AGATHA *to* U.C.) Hullo, Len.

LEN. Oh, hullo.

> (AGATHA *glances knowingly at* LEN.)

MARISA. I have to see to the tables.

LEN. I'll come and help you.

> (MARISA *goes out* D.R., *followed by* LEN. DORA *looks after them.* AGATHA *moves downstage a little.*)

AGATHA. You like 'im, don't you?

DORA. Who?

AGATHA. 'im!

DORA (*casually*). He's all right. (*Breaks* U.S.)

AGATHA. That all you think about 'im?

DORA. He only came here last night. I don't know 'im very well.

AGATHA. I see. (*Pause.*) I can't think why you young girls are always so keen on men, anyhow. They bring nothing but trouble. (*Sits* R. *of table* L.C., *takes out her knitting from beach bag.*)

DORA. Don't you approve of marriage?

AGATHA. Approve of it? I'd like to lay my 'ands on the man who invented it. Mark my words, Dora, never get married if you're a woman. Men—they're all the same—idle and good-for-nothing. And my 'arold was the worst of the lot. He never did a full day's work if 'alf would do.

DORA (*down to* U.R. *of* AGATHA's *chair*). I expect he knew how lucky he was to be married to you.

AGATHA. He should 'ave done. I told him often enough. There were two things in his life—beer and football—and he 'ad too much of both.

DORA. Why ever didn't you leave him?

AGATHA (*with simple logic*). Leave 'im? I was married to 'im.

(MR. MALLET *comes in from the archway. He is comparatively cheerful. He comes* C.)

MALLET. Oh, dear! I must have overslept! A lovely morning like this, too. I suppose I'm too late for breakfast?

DORA. I'll go and see, shall I?

MALLET. Oh, would you? That's ever so kind of you. Perhaps you could hustle me up a cup of coffee, eh?

DORA. I'll try. (DORA *goes out* D.R.)

MALLET. Well, Mrs. Hepworth, I feel I'm in your debt.

AGATHA. 'ow do you mean?

MALLET. Well, thanks to you I spent a very good night.

AGATHA. I beg your pardon?

MALLET. It was you who suggested I ask them to find me a room for the night. Don't you remember?

AGATHA. Oh, yes. So I did. You weren't able to contact any of your party, then?

MALLET. No. I tried to telephone them at Viareggio—that's the place they're due at according to the itinerary—but nobody seemed to know anything about them.

AGATHA. You don't seem very upset.

MALLET. Well, I suddenly thought "what's the good of getting upset"? It was silly, wasn't it? Wasn't it silly? You see, if I hadn't got lost I would never have seen this place, and to tell you the truth I rather like it. I shall have such fun exploring it today.

AGATHA. Yes, I'm sure you will.

MALLET. I say you're just starting your holiday, too, aren't you?

AGATHA. I was 'oping to, yes.

MALLET. Then we can explore together! That would be jolly, wouldn't it? Wouldn't that be jolly?

AGATHA (*rising*). You'll 'ave to excuse me, Mr. Mallet—

MALLET (*restraining her*). Don't go, Mrs. Hepworth—

AGATHA. I 'ave to.

MALLET. Oh, I see. You're afraid your husband might appear?

AGATHA. You'd 'ave a shock if he did!

(JULIAN WHITTLE *comes in through the french windows. As usual, he is very hot. He comes to between them.*)

WHITTLE. Good morning, everyone.

AGATHA (*beaming*). You're the very person I was 'oping to see!

WHITTLE. Am I?

MALLET. I hope you didn't think I was being—er—forward with your wife.

WHITTLE. What are you talking about?

MALLET. Aren't you Mr. Hepworth?

WHITTLE (*vehemently*). Good God, no! (*To* AGATHA.) I beg your pardon, I didn't mean—

AGATHA. This is Mr. Whittle. Any worries, queries, problems, and he'll answer them. Won't you?

WHITTLE. If I can. If I can. (*To* MALLET.) But you aren't one of mine, are you? You aren't with Eagle?

MALLET. No. I'm Progressive.

WHITTLE. Oh. Out of my province, I'm afraid. Sorry. (*Turns away and comes face to face with* AGATHA.)

AGATHA. I thought perhaps you could stretch a point and 'elp 'im.

WHITTLE. I'd be in terrible trouble with Head Office.

AGATHA. But he's English!

WHITTLE. My dear madam, I am the Eagle Tourist Representative not the British Consul. (*To* MALLET.) Haven't you got a representative of Progressive out here?

MALLET. I'm not supposed to be here. I got left behind by the coach at Monte Carlo.

WHITTLE. That was careless. (*Crosses below* MALLET *to chair* L. *of table* R.C.)

MALLET. Yes, it was, wasn't it? Wasn't it careless? I managed to get here and they found me a room for the night.

WHITTLE. You were lucky. Later in the season they'd have been full up.

(*Enter* DORA *with a glass of orange juice.*)

DORA. Marisa says there is no coffee left, so I've brought you some orange juice.

WHITTLE (*taking it*). Oh, thank you, Miss Cowley. How very thoughtful. (*Sits* L. *of table* R.C. *and drinks.*) Delicious!

(MALLET *watches* WHITTLE *as he enjoys the orange drink.* DORA *enjoys the situation and moves above* WHITTLE *to seat* U.C.)

Well, Mr. Mallet, I don't really see how I can help you—

AGATHA (*to* L. *of* WHITTLE). You can at least listen to him!

WHITTLE (*rising and edging from her*). Oh—yes, yes, I suppose I can. But what I really came about, Mrs. Hepworth, is your green form. I should have collected it yesterday, but what with one thing and another it slipped my mind.

(MALLET *perches nervously on the edge of the chair* R. *of table* R.C.)

AGATHA. Oh, we gave the form to the hotel.

WHITTLE. No, no, that was the pink. The pink goes to the hotel. The green goes to me.

AGATHA. I don't think we've got a green.

WHITTLE (*laughing nervously*). But you must have a green. Everyone's got a green. That is, everyone with Eagle. And you are with Eagle, aren't you, Mrs. Hepworth?

AGATHA. Oh, yes, we're with Eagle all right—

WHITTLE. Then you must have a green form. Without it there's no proof that you've paid.

AGATHA. No proof that I've paid! I 'ope you're not getting nasty, Mr. Whittle.

WHITTLE. No, no, Mrs. Hepworth—of course not—

AGATHA. I'll go and 'ave a look in our room. But let me tell you this, Mr. Whittle—if I can't find it, I've no intention of paying again— oh, dear me, no!—and I don't advise you to try and make me!

(AGATHA *pounds off upstairs.* WHITTLE *sits exhausted and takes some more orange,* MALLET *rises and comes to* L. *of* WHITTLE.)

MALLET. Mr. Whittle—(WHITTLE *jumps.*)—perhaps I'd better tell you the whole story from the beginning.

WHITTLE (*rises and moves away* R. *below the table and circles above it,* MALLET *following*). Oh, well, I'm afraid I'm rather busy at the moment—

MALLET. But Mrs. Hepworth said you'd listen to me.

WHITTLE (*loudly*). I don't care what Mrs. Hep-. (*Softly.*) I don't care what Mrs. Hepworth said. She is not my mistress.

(*Realizes what he has said.* MALLET *and* DORA *laugh.*)

MALLET. Couldn't you spare just a few minutes?

WHITTLE. Mr. Mallet, I am not the Missing Persons Bureau!

MALLET. You see, we met at Victoria at 22.15, and departed Victoria at—

WHITTLE. I have to see the proprietor, so if you'll excuse me—

MALLET (*cheerfully*). I'll come with you, then we can talk as we go! (*Following* WHITTLE *off.*) It was all okay up to then, you see. We left Victoria as expected at 22.45 hours. We arrived at Newhaven—

      (WHITTLE *stumbles out through the archway, pursued by* MALLET, *still talking.*

      FIONA *comes in from upstairs. She is holding herself very carefully, as if afraid that she might collapse at any moment.*)

DORA. 'ullo. You feeling better?

FIONA. Yes, thank you, dear. (*Sits* R. *of table* L.C.) I had a little lay down and washed my face and I feel quite different.

DORA. Oh, good.

FIONA. Agatha's carrying on like a thing possessed up there—turning out all drawers!—so I thought I'd come down here. Seems more peaceful. Everyone gone on to the beach, dear?

DORA (*to above table* L.C.). No. That Mr. Barrett's in the dining-room with Marisa.

FIONA. Ooh! I say, he does work fast.

DORA. Yes. He does, doesn't he?

                 (*Pause.*)

FIONA (*thoughtfully*). It's a funny thing, isn't it?

DORA. What is?

FIONA. Sex. You know.

DORA. Oh—

FIONA. Well, you must 'ave 'eard of it.

DORA. Oh, I've 'eard of it, but I don't know it.

FIONA. I mean, some people go in for it, and others just don't seem to fancy it, somehow.

DORA (*thoughtfully*). No.

                (*A pause.*)

    Did you ever fancy it?

FIONA. Oh no, dear. It never appealed to me, somehow. I 'ad better things to do with my time when I was young, I can tell you. And it wasn't for lack of chances, either.

DORA. I'm sure it wasn't. I bet you were ever so pretty.

FIONA. Well, I wasn't bad, though I say it as shouldn't.

DORA. I wonder if I'll ever get married.

FIONA. 'course you will, dear. If you want to, that is.

DORA. Oh, I want to.

FIONA. I expect you meet a lot of nice boys on your bus?

DORA. Oh, yes. But they never want to go beyond the threepenny fare stage. And anyway, the boys I like always seem to go for girls who aren't like me. They prefer the more flashy type—you know. (*With a look towards the dining-room.*)

FIONA. I wouldn't worry, dear. You've plenty of time. If you want to get married you will.

DORA. P'raps we both will.

FIONA. Oh, not me, dear. I'm redundant.

(WHITTLE *comes in from the archway followed by* MALLET, *still in full spate.*)

MALLET. . . . and I can't understand how I came to miss the coach. It's not a thing you expect to happen, is it? I mean, you might expect a bit of rain or something like that—but miss the coach—it's such a silly thing to do. Isn't it silly?

WHITTLE. Yes, Mr. Mallet, I'm sure that's very interesting.

MALLET. Perhaps you'd like to check my itinerary?

WHITTLE (*arriving* C., MALLET *on his* R.). No, thank you. Good morning, Miss Francis. Not out in the sun?

FIONA. I 'aven't been well, Julian.

WHITTLE. Oh dear, what was the trouble?

FIONA. I expect it was that fricassee of chicken we 'ad last night.

WHITTLE. But you're feeling better now?

FIONA. Oh, yes, thank you.

(AGATHA *pounds in, brandishing a cricket bat.*)

AGATHA. 'ere! Look what I've found!

DORA (*to* D.L. *of table* L.C.). Where did you get that from, Mrs. Hepworth?

AGATHA. I think it belongs to that little boy with ginger hair. 'e left in on the landing.

FIONA (*piously*). That's stealing.

AGATHA. It's what?

FIONA. Stealing.

AGATHA. Oh, blimey! Talk sense! I've borrowed it, that's all—borrowed it! 'e can 'ave it back this afternoon. He's a nasty little boy, anyway. Well, I gather you're feeling better.

FIONA. I was just telling Julian that I expect it was that frisakee of chicken that upset me.

AGATHA. You didn't 'ave any.

FIONA. No, but I saw it.

AGATHA. But you didn't feel ill until this morning.

FIONA. The more I thought about it the worse I felt.

AGATHA. Yes, and the more I think about you the worse I feel! You any good at cricket, Mr. Whittle?

WHITTLE. I'm afraid I'm much too busy—

AGATHA. Whatever work you've got to do you can do this afternoon. It's part of your job to see that we enjoy ourselves, isn't it?

WHITTLE. Well, yes, but—

AGATHA. Right! Then you're playing cricket!

WHITTLE. Did you find the green form, Mrs. Hepworth?

AGATHA. No. (*Waving the cricket bat.*) I found this instead! What about you, Mr. Mallet? You any good with bat and ball?

MALLET. I was just telling Mr. Whittle about how I—

AGATHA. You can do that when you're fielding. I should think you're a born silly mid-off.

> (LEN *comes in glumly from* D.R. AGATHA *marches across to him.*)

Aaah! You're just the man we need, Len. You can open the bowling. (*She drags him across to join* WHITTLE *and* MALLET.)

LEN. Oh no, look 'ere. I'm not—

AGATHA. Now, Fiona, you got your hat?

FIONA. Yes, Agatha.

AGATHA. Well, get it on. We don't want you catching sunstroke on top of everything else. Oh, I am going to enjoy myself! You ready, Dora? Off we go!

> (AGATHA, *cricket bat waving, starts to herd them off enthusiastically to the beach.*)

Fiona, come along!

FIONA. I'd better just get my *Woman's Own*.

AGATHA. For once in your life you'll 'ave to do without Beverley Nichols!

QUICK CURTAIN

SCENE 2

Before lunch the same day. The stage is empty. HUBBACK *and* MALLET *come on slowly from the beach. They both look very hot and exhausted. They sit in silence (*HUBBACK L. *of table* R.C.; MALLET R. *of table* L.C.) *and sigh with relief. After a while* HUBBACK *speaks.*

HUBBACK. How the hell she managed to find us I'll never know! The wife and I had no sooner settled ourselves when all of a sudden there she was, beaming all over her face, bearing down on us, like some friendly tank.

MALLET. I expect she thought you were interested in cricket.

HUBBACK. I am interested. Nobody more so. But when it comes to being asked to play, well that's a different matter entirely.

MALLET. I must say, I feel quite exhausted. You see, I never really fancied myself as a googly bowler.

HUBBACK. No, I must say you weren't very impressive.

MALLET. Considering I hadn't played since I was at school I thought I did pretty well.

HUBBACK. Yes, of course. (*He chuckles to himself.*)

MALLET (*rising, slightly resentful*). I don't think I like your attitude.

HUBBACK. I'm sorry. Didn't mean to be rude. (*Pause.*) But one has one's standards, after all.

MALLET. I didn't notice you bowling all that well, Brigadier!

HUBBACK (*casually*). Well, of course not. I'm a batsman, really.

MALLET. I would never have guessed it. (*Resumes his seat.*)

(*A pause.* HUBBACK *turns and looks at him.*)

HUBBACK. I beg your pardon?

MALLET. I said I would never have guessed that you were a batsman.

HUBBACK (*with great restraint*). Are you trying to be offensive?

MALLET. From the way you held the bat I should have thought you were more used to playing rounders!

HUBBACK. Well, now of course you're being deliberately rude. Perhaps it would be better if we discontinued the conversation. (*Turns away.*)

MALLET. It's a pity if you can't face the truth.

HUBBACK (*rising angrily*). It is not the truth! I did extremely well. I knocked five!

(LEN *comes in through the french windows to* C., *between them.*)

LEN. Hullo, hullo! what's all this about, then? It's only a game, after all!

(HUBBACK *and* MALLET *both turn to look at* LEN.)

HUBBACK. It may only be a game, Barrett, but if you play a game you should play it seriously or not at all. A little more attention from you wouldn't have been amiss, either.

LEN. What do you mean?

HUBBACK. Whenever a ball came anywhere near you you were always gazing at some pretty girl on the beach.

LEN. Who wants to run after a ball with all them birds about?

HUBBACK. Then you shouldn't have played.

LEN. I didn't have any choice, if you remember. Any more than you did.

MALLET. Even so I do feel that having agreed to play—

LEN. I never agreed! I was shanghaied.

MALLET. Well, having been shanghaied, you should have taken it more seriously. It's only sporting.

HUBBACK. Quite right!

(MALLET *looks surprised.*)

I must say, Mallet, I agree with you entirely.

MALLET. You do?

HUBBACK. Certainly. You know, you would have had a couple of wickets if this blighter had been ready for a catch.

MALLET (*pleased*). You think so?

HUBBACK. Absolutely certain of it!

LEN. Go on! They were miles away. (*Breaks* U.S. *to corner seat, facing away.*)

HUBBACK. It was you who was miles away. You ask Whittle. After all, he was umpiring.

(WHITTLE *comes in. He is very hot and is mopping his brow. Around his waist is a woollen sweater umpire-fashion. He comes to* U.L. *of* HUBBACK.)

Ah, Whittle, you're the chap who can settle this. I say that young Barrett missed a couple of decent chances off Mallet's bowling.

WHITTLE. Well, I must say, one was an absolute sitter! How you came to miss it, my dear fellow, I shall never know. I'd already raised my finger to give 'Out' and Miss Francis was half-way back to the beach hut. (*Crosses to door* D.R.)

LEN (*downstage a little*). I didn't see it.

HUBBACK. I should think you didn't. Looking the other way, that's why.

WHITTLE (*calling offstage*). Marisa! (*Sits chair* R. *of table* R.C.) This sun really is getting me down.

LEN. At least you didn't have to run after the flamin' ball. I wish I'd been the umpire.

WHITTLE. I can assure you it's an extremely arduous task standing out there in the heat and bearing the responsibility for making the correct decisions.

MALLET. But you didn't always make the correct decisions, did you?

WHITTLE. I most certainly did.

MALLET. What about that time you gave Mrs. Hepworth out l.b.w.? We all disagreed with you.

HUBBACK. What does it matter? She refused to be given out, anyway.

(MARISA *comes in* D.R.)

WHITTLE. Ah, Marisa. I'd like a long orange and soda.

MARISA. You have a good morning on the beach?

HUBBACK. Oh, very good, thank you.

MARISA. You swam in the sea and kept cool?

WHITTLE. No. We ran on the beach and got hot.

MARISA. Of course. I forget. The English are very sportive. (*She goes out* D.R.)

HUBBACK. Yes. Yes, I suppose we are, really.

(AGATHA *and* MRS. H. *come in together, arm-in-arm.* MRS. H. *carries the cricket bat. They are both cheerful. The men watch them in silence as they pass down* C., *below table* L.C. *to* D.L.)

AGATHA. Well, I must say, Mrs. 'ubback, you did well! I never thought you 'ad it in you.

MRS. H. One mustn't always go by outside appearances, you know.

AGATHA. I was surprised enough when you hit that first ball for six, but later on you took two beautiful catches as well!

MRS. H. Well, I didn't play square leg at Cheltenham Ladies College for nothing, you know.

AGATHA. Oh, I thought you must 'ave played before, dear. I could tell. You 'ad style. You know what I mean? (*She sits* MRS. H. *in chair* D.L. *and pulls chair from* L. *of table* L.C. *to face her.*) I bet you're feeling better, too, aren't you?

MRS. H. Better?

AGATHA. You was feeling a bit dicky this morning, don't you remember?

MRS. H. Oh, yes, of course. I'm much better now, thank you.

AGATHA. Knew you would be! Nothing like a nice bit of exercise to put the roses back. I'm glad we've got to know each other so quickly, aren't you, dear? I don't mind telling you, I wasn't very 'opeful about you at first.

MRS. H. Oh. Weren't you?

AGATHA. No. I took one look and I said to myself, "She's stuck up, she is:" Stuck up, indeed! When I think of you out there on the beach this morning! And I'll tell you one thing—now that we're team-mates you can call me Agatha.

MRS. H. (*a trifle reluctant*). Oh—very well.

AGATHA. And what's your name, dear?

MRS. H. Er—Audrey.

AGATHA. Then I shall call you Audrey! Audrey and Agatha! (*Turns to face the men.*) Isn't that nice? You boys are very quiet. Don't tell me you're tired?

WHITTLE (*weakly*). No, no, of course not, Mrs. Hepworth.

AGATHA. You all feeling better for your exercise? Yes, I can see you are! I reckon you're proud of your Audrey, aren't you, Captain?

HUBBACK. I'm a little surprised.

AGATHA (*moving to* C., *wagging a finger at him playfully*). But we were very naughty, weren't we?

HUBBACK. Were we?

AGATHA. Yes, we were. We crept away and hid ourselves, didn't we? You should 'ave seen them, Len. They'd got behind the biggest sun-shade I've ever seen! But I spotted Audrey's shoes peeping out. It was that that gave you away.

HUBBACK (*grimly*). Oh, was it? (*Glares at* MRS. H.)

AGATHA. I bet you thought I wouldn't find you, eh?

WHITTLE. He should have known better.

(MARISA *comes in with* WHITTLE's *drink*.)

AGATHA. 'ullo, Marisa! *Buon giorno.* (*To below table* R.C.) Who's that for, dear?

MARISA (D.R. *of* WHITTLE). For Mr. Whittle.

AGATHA. Then let me 'ave it. Mr. Whittle won't mind. (*Takes the drink.*) I think Audrey could do with this. (*Hands it to* MRS. H.) There you are, dear. I reckon you deserve it.

MRS. H. (*to* AGATHA). Thank you very much.

WHITTLE. Don't mention it.

MARISA. You are all going to the dancing tonight?

LEN (*eagerly to above table* R.C.). What dancing is that?

MARISA. Tonight there is dancing and music in the streets. There will be many people there to see the lights and the fireworks and to listen to the music. It is all very gay.

LEN. It sounds fun. (*Round to* R. *of* MARISA.) Are you going, Marisa?

MARISA. Er—oh, yes. I shall be there.

LEN. Perhaps we can go together.

AGATHA. We'll all go, Len! (MARISA *smiles at* AGATHA *and goes off* D.R. LEN *wanders* D.R., *watching her go.*) Do we need tickets or anything, Mr. Whittle?

WHITTLE (*rising*). Oh, no. Just follow the noise. You can't miss it. (*Up to the archway.*) Well, I really must be off. I have work to do.

AGATHA. That's right, Mr. Whittle. We mustn't keep you from your work, must we?

(WHITTLE *turns to give her a look and finds that* MALLET *has come up and is next to him.*)

WHITTLE. What do you want?

MALLET. I'll come down with you part of the way.

WHITTLE. That's quite all right. I'm sure I can manage.

MALLET. But I haven't finished telling you about how I got lost.

WHITTLE. Haven't you?

MALLET. Oh, no! There's a lot more yet.

WHITTLE. I was afraid there might be. But you don't want to miss your lunch, do you?

MALLET. There's about ten minutes to go before lunch. Now, where had I got to?

WHITTLE. I think you were in the middle of the English Channel.

MALLET. That's right.

(They start to go.)

Well, everything went according to the time-table and we reached Dieppe at 15.30 hours. We were due to leave Dieppe at 16.00 hours, but they told us there would be a slight delay.

(MALLET continues inexorably as he follows WHITTLE off through the archway.
AGATHA crosses to C.)

AGATHA. Well, now, I think this afternoon we'd better all 'ave a little rest.

(They all look astonished. LEN moves onstage a little, MRS. H. rises and HUBBACK rises to R of AGATHA.)

HUBBACK. You don't mean it?

AGATHA. Yes, I do, General. We must save a bit of energy for tonight, mustn't we?

HUBBACK. Tonight?

AGATHA. For the festival, of course. We'll all 'ave to go to that!

(LEN moves away R.; HUBBACK crosses AGATHA to D.L.)

LEN. Oh, do you think so?

AGATHA. Yes, I do think so, Len. Young chap like you ought to be glad to go dancing.

LEN. Well, yes, I am, but—*(Glancing towards where MARISA went off.)*

AGATHA. That's all right, then. We're going!

(Enter DORA from the beach.)

Oh, there you are, Dora. Thought you were going to miss your lunch.

DORA. I just stopped to buy some more sun-oil.

AGATHA. Oh, dear! Did I use a lot of it this morning?

DORA. It's all right. It would have gone soon anyway.

AGATHA. We've just been 'earing about the festival tonight. Did you know about that?

DORA. Yes, I did see something.

AGATHA. You'll be going, of course?

DORA. Well, I don't know.

AGATHA *(turning to LEN)*. I tell you what! Len—

LEN (*quickly*). I think I'll go and have a wash before lunch. Excuse me!
(*He goes off hurriedly upstairs.*)

AGATHA. He's in a 'urry.

DORA (*a little embarrassed*). What do you expect? (*Crosses below* AGATHA
to D.R.C.)

(HUBBACK *and* MRS. H. *are talking to each other* D.L.)

AGATHA (*to* L. *of* DORA). What do you mean?

DORA. Mrs. Hepworth, you weren't going to tell him to take me,
were you?

AGATHA. Yes. Why not?

DORA. He doesn't want to!

AGATHA. I'll make him want to.

DORA. You can't do that, Mrs. Hepworth.

AGATHA. Why not?

DORA. It wouldn't be the same, somehow.

AGATHA (*logically*). You 'aven't much time, you know, if you're going
'ome on Friday.

DORA. I know. But he doesn't seem to notice me.

AGATHA. 'ere, I'll go and—!

DORA (*stopping her again*). No!

AGATHA. I could do it, you know.

DORA. Yes, I know you could do it, Mrs. Hepworth.

AGATHA. You've quite made up your mind, 'aven't you?

DORA. Yes. I have. (*She sits* R. *of table* D.R.)

AGATHA. All right, love. I won't say anything.

DORA (*doubtfully*). Promise?

AGATHA. Promise. (*She turns and speaks loudly to include the* HUBBACKS.)
Well, I suppose we'd better go and have a tidy, eh, Audrey? (*Compact out.*) I bet I look a mess. Ooooh! 'aven't I caught the sun! If
I'm like this after one morning, 'eaven knows what I'll be like at the
end of the fortnight!

HUBBACK. You're staying a fortnight, then, Mrs. Hepworth?

AGATHA. Well, you know—"15 days 'oliday—12 nights at resort". By
then I shall be like a Red Indian, I should think. And just about as
reserved, eh, General? (*She laughs loudly.*)

(AGATHA *goes off upstairs.* HUBBACK *presses bell-push* D.L.)

HUBBACK. "Audrey and Agatha!"

MRS. H. I hadn't any choice, had I, Charles?

HUBBACK. You seemed to be getting on like a house on fire. You came
in like a couple of old school friends. And another thing—you never
told me you played cricket.

MRS. H. (*crossing him to* C.). You never asked.

HUBBACK. I wish you'd said so before.

MRS. H. What possible difference could it have made?

HUBBACK. Well, if I'd known you were interested in cricket—

MRS. H. I'm not interested in it. I hate the game. But I was damned if I was going to let that woman show me up! (*She goes off.*)

(DORA *giggles.*)

HUBBACK. Well, I'm blowed!

(WHITTLE *comes in, breathless, from the french windows. He comes to* C.)

WHITTLE. I think I've managed to give him the slip.

HUBBACK. How on earth did you do that?

WHITTLE. I went into the gents on the corner and came out over the back wall. As far as I know he's still waiting outside!

HUBBACK. He may come back here to find you.

WHITTLE (*sitting* R. *of table* L.C., *mopping his brow.*). I hope not! I expect he'll think I've gone on into the village and try to find me there.

HUBBACK. But he doesn't know his way around. He may get lost.

WHITTLE. He's lost already, so it won't matter, will it?

(*Enter* MARISA D.R.)

MARISA. You rang, signor?

HUBBACK. Yes. Large pink gin, please. And what about you, Whittle? You deserve something after your athletics.

WHITTLE. That's very decent of you. Sherry, please.

HUBBACK. How about you, Miss Cowley?

DORA. Oh. No, thanks.

(*Exit* MARISA D.R.)

HUBBACK. You'll have to give me a few lessons in escape tactics. Mine weren't very successful this morning.

WHITTLE. I would have thought it would have been easy for you, sir— military man and all that.

HUBBACK. Yes, but I rather underestimated the opposition.

WHITTLE. You going to this festival thing tonight?

HUBBACK. I expect Mrs. Hepworth will insist.

DORA. It sounds like a lot of fun.

WHITTLE. Have you ever been to one of these things?

DORA. Yes. I went on Tuesday. I shall go again tonight though. After all, it'll be my last chance. 'Rene and me go home on Friday.

HUBBACK. Do you think she'll be well enough to go tonight?

DORA. Shouldn't think so. I expect I'll go on my own.

HUBBACK. Well, pretty girl like you won't have much trouble finding a young man to dance with.

DORA. Oh, there are plenty of Italian boys. But they all keep asking you things in Italian and pretending they don't understand when you say no.

(MARISA *comes in with drinks on a small tray.* HUBBACK *pulls chair* L. *of table* L.C. *to its original position and sits.*)

HUBBACK. Thank you, m'dear.

MARISA. *Prego.*

HUBBACK. You going to this affair tonight, Marisa?

MARISA. When I have finished here.

(DORA *looks a little regretful.*)

WHITTLE. Marisa dances like a dream, you know, Brigadier.

HUBBACK. I'm sure she does.

(MR. MALLET *rushes on through the french windows. He sees* WHITTLE.)

MALLET. Oh, there you are! I thought you couldn't still be where I left you!

WHITTLE. Oh, my God! (*Rises hurriedly.*) Excuse me. (*He rushes off through the archway and out of the main door.*)

MALLET. But, Mr. Whittle, I hadn't finished telling you about Monte Carlo—! (*He chases off after* WHITTLE.)

MARISA (*bewildered*). What was that?

HUBBACK. Oh, just a little counter-offensive.

(MARISA *is about to go, when* LEN *runs in from the archway and almost collides with her. They meet below corner seat* U.C.)

LEN. Oh—sorry!

MARISA. You are running for your lunch?

LEN. No. I'm running for my life.

HUBBACK. Mrs. Hepworth?

LEN. Yes. She spotted me as I was getting into the lift, but I just got the door shut in time. Then she tried to beat me to it by running down the stairs, but I won by a short head.

(AGATHA *pounds in, breathless and beaming to* R. *of* LEN.)

AGATHA (*to* LEN). I very nearly beat you, you know! You were just closing the lift gate as I got there.

LEN. I'm so sorry. I didn't see you.

AGATHA. That's all right, dear. Well, now, I bet you're all ready for your lunches, aren't you? 'ave you seen my sister, Marisa? I thought she'd be up in our room 'aving a lay down, but she isn't.

MARISA. I have not seen her, Mrs. Hepworth.

LEN. I don't think she came back from the beach, did she?

AGATHA. Oh, yes, she came back all right. Where did she go when you got back from the village, Dora?

DORA. She wasn't here when I got back, don't you remember?

AGATHA. But she was with you.

DORA. She wasn't, you know.

AGATHA. 'course she was, dear. She went into the village with you. Said she'd meet me back 'ere.

DORA. But I went into the village on my own.

AGATHA (*to above table* R.C.). Dora, just as you was leaving the beach she said she'd like to go into the village, so I told her to catch you up and go with you. I knew you wouldn't mind. You mean she never caught you up?

DORA. No. I never saw her after I left the beach.

AGATHA. Then where is she now?

DORA. Well—I don't know.

AGATHA (*away below chair* R. *of table* L.C.). Oh, blimey! She might be anywhere!

HUBBACK. Well, surely she'll find her way back here all right?

AGATHA. You don't know Fiona like what I do. I know what she's like. She couldn't cross the road without me to show her how! Anything might 'ave 'appened to her! I only let her out of my sight because I thought she was going with Dora 'ere! (*Suddenly and unexpectedly she dissolves into tears.*) Ooooh! What 'ave I done? What 'ave I done? She might be dead! And it'll all be my fault! Ooooh!

> (*She sits and the others crowd around with words of comfort.* HUBBACK *to* D.L. *of the table;* MARISA *to* U.L. *of her;* DORA *and* LEN *to her* R.)

HUBBACK		Now, now! You mustn't feel like that!
DORA		I'm sure she'll turn up all right, Mrs. Hep-
	(*together*).	worth.
LEN		It isn't your fault, you know.
MRS. H.		Don't upset yourself, Mrs. Hepworth.

AGATHA. I'm a wicked, wicked woman! It was my responsibility. She's stupid, you see. She's got no more brain than she was born with. She won't 'ave the sense to go to the police; and if she does they'll probably arrest her! Colonel, you'd better organize a search party.

HUBBACK (*blinking*). Search party?

AGATHA (*snapping*). You know what a search party is, don't you?

HUBBACK. Of course!

AGATHA. Well, arrange one! (*Softening into tears again.*) How could she do it, Dora? Getting herself lost like this.

DORA. She might not be lost, Mrs. Hepworth. We'll find her.

HUBBACK. She'll probably come walking in at any minute as right as rain.

AGATHA (*loudly*). If she does I'll kill 'er! (*Wilting again.*) She's dead, I know she is! We'd better get the police, Marisa dear.

MARISA. But, Mrs. Hepworth—

AGATHA (*to* HUBBACK). You organized that search party yet, General?

HUBBACK. Well, no, I—

AGATHA (*snapping*). Get on with it, then! (*Rises and moves* U.S. *towards· the archway.*) Oh, Fiona! Where are you, love? Where are you?

> (WHITTLE *comes running in from the archway, with* MALLET *in hot pursuit.*)

(*Seeing them.*) Ooooh!!

> WHITTLE *and* MALLET *run down* C. *and are making for the door* D.R. *as*

THE CURTAIN FALLS.

ACT THREE

The same evening. It is dark outside and the electric lights are on. The curtains are still open, so that we can see the night sky and various lanterns, etc., which decorate the outside of the hotel. Occasionally we hear snatches of music from a nearby restaurant.

When the curtain rises MRS. HUBBACK *is sitting* L. *of table* R.C., *sipping her after-dinner coffee and glancing through a magazine.*

DORA is at the windows gazing out rather disconsolately. A cup of coffee stands untouched on the table L.C.

MRS. H. I should have your coffee if I were you. It'll get cold.

DORA (*coming to*). Oh—yes. I forgot. (*She drinks the coffee and makes a face.*) They're getting ready for the fireworks out there. I suppose we'll miss all that now.

MRS. H. There's nothing to stop you going if you want to.

DORA. Well, it wouldn't seem very kind, would it? Not with Miss Francis still missing and everything.

MRS. H. There's nothing you can do. Anyhow, I don't know what all the fuss is about. There's nothing to prevent her going off on her own for a few hours if she wants to. She is over twenty-one, after all.

DORA. You would 'ave thought she would 'ave telephoned or something.

MRS. H. Have you ever tried to telephone in this country? There are as many hazards as an obstacle race. Frankly, I think Miss Francis is to be congratulated.

DORA. Why?

MRS. H. She's succeeded in doing the one thing the rest of us have been trying to do all day—escape from Mrs. Hepworth.

DORA (*wide-eyed*). You don't think she's done it deliberately?

MRS. H. I wouldn't be surprised.

DORA. P'raps she's been taken ill again. She wasn't very well this morning, remember.

MRS. H. Well, the whole town is being turned inside out to find her so she's bound to turn up soon. The police are out in force—looking like something out of Gilbert and Sullivan in those ridiculous hats—Mr. Whittle and Mr. Barrett are down there on a house-to-house search; and practically every male holidaymaker in the vicinity has been roped in for the hunt.

DORA. I must say the Brigadier's working very hard.

MRS. H. He's having the time of his life! I don't think he's had so much fun since he organized the Home Guard.

DORA (*returning to the window*). Well, I 'ope they find her soon.

> (HUBBACK *bustles in from the main entrance. He is hot and businesslike. He carries a large piece of cardboard and a piece of tree hewn vaguely in the shape of an officer's baton. He is wearing his panama hat.*)

HUBBACK (*proudly*). Well, we've got the whole town sealed off. She can't possibly get away.

MRS. H. How do you know she's trying to get away?

HUBBACK. You know what I mean. (*Turns the cardboard round on which he has drawn a large map in various colours.*) Take a look at this! (*Places it across the chair* R. *of table* L.C. *and stands on* R. *of it.*) This might interest you, too, Miss Cowley.

> (DORA *comes down* L. *and peers at it disinterestedly.*)

(*Proudly.*) There! Recognize it?

MRS. H. (*after looking closely*). Is it anybody I know?

HUBBACK. It's a detailed plan of the area!

MRS. H. Oh, I see.

HUBBACK (*pointing with his stick*). All this is the sea.

MRS. H. Then why have you marked it in red?

HUBBACK. For the sake of clarity.

MRS. H. It hardly makes it clear if you mark the sea in red, dear. Most misleading, I would have thought. Blue would have been nice.

HUBBACK. I've already used the blue for something else.

MRS. H. Then you shouldn't have done, Charles. Don't you agree, Miss Cowley?

DORA (*who isn't paying attention*). H'm?

MRS. H. The sea—what colour would you have used for the sea?

DORA. Oh—blue, of course!

MRS. H. There you are, Charles.

DORA (*logically*). I mean the sea is blue, isn't it?

HUBBACK. I don't give a damn what colour the sea is! My sea is red!

MRS. H. Really, Charles, there's no need to get excited. We're only trying to keep you straight on the details.

HUBBACK (*patiently*). Look, I know the sea is blue. But for the sake of this map the sea is red. All right?

MRS. H. All right, dear. If that's the way you want it. It's inaccurate, though.

HUBBACK (*firmly*). This is the sea.

> (*She smiles at him and says nothing.*)

Now, this is the railway running at the back of the village, and these bits marked in yellow are the hills.

DORA. In yellow?

HUBBACK. In yellow. (*He looks at* MRS. H.)

MRS. H. I didn't say anything, dear.

HUBBACK. This is the main road.

DORA. It looks like a river.

HUBBACK. I don't care what it looks like. It's the main road. This is the line of beach huts on the sands.

MRS. H. (*thoughtfully*). Yellow would have been lovely for the sands.

HUBBACK. The sands are green.

MRS. H. How absurd.

HUBBACK. Do you want me to explain this to you or not?

MRS. H. Yes, of course, Charles. I'm sorry. I won't interrupt again.

HUBBACK. Good. This is the ruined church in the old part of the town, and over here is the Cafe Romana where they have the Roof Garden. All this area is being combed by the local police. Over here are the chaps from the Miramar Hotel under a fellow called Phipps. And meeting up with them from the north is a group under a chap named Humbolt.

DORA. Where are Len and Mr. Whittle?

HUBBACK. They're somewhere over here.

MRS. H. In the green sand.

HUBBACK. Precisely. They're working along the beach to meet up with the left flank of the Miramar Hotel. Then they'll continue down through the centre of the town and back to base.

MRS. H. Where's that?

HUBBACK. That's here.

MRS. H. Oh, yes, of course.

HUBBACK. So we've got virtually four prongs to the attack—A here; B—here; C—over there; and D—down the bottom there.

MRS. H. And where are you?

HUBBACK. I'm sitting in H.Q. over here. (*Gestures.*)

MRS. H. What? That nasty little brown smudge?

HUBBACK. If everything goes according to plan the Group Commanders will be back here within an hour and Miss Francis will be in the net. (*Takes the map upstage and puts it down on the corner seat.*)

MRS. H. In the net? You make her sound like a prawn.

HUBBACK (*to above table* L.C.). I suppose I ought to go and put Mrs. Hepworth in the picture. Do you know where she is?

MRS. H. Well, she wasn't down for dinner. You know, I'm afraid she really is rather upset.

HUBBACK. Yes. Most surprising to see her react in that way, really. You know—tears and all that. Never thought she had it in her. Give her full marks for that.

(AGATHA *comes in from upstairs. She is wearing an over-elaborate silk dinner dress of a suitably sombre colour. She is sniffling occasionally into her handkerchief. She comes to* C.)

AGATHA. I suppose there's no news of Fiona?

HUBBACK. Not yet, I'm afraid.

AGATHA. I just can't forgive myself. Whatever's 'appened to 'er, Audrey, it's all my fault. She didn't want to come 'ere in the first place. I made her! I said it was good for her.

HUBBACK. And you were right.

AGATHA (*snapping*). You call this good for her? Nothing like this ever 'appened to her at Eastcliffe—never! It was me—I made her come out 'ere to her doom!

HUBBACK (*to* L. *of* AGATHA *at* C.). Nothing's happened to her, Mrs. Hepworth. Everything possible is being done to find her, and you can rest assured that she'll turn up all right very soon.

AGATHA. May be I drove her away with the things I said. I'm a murderess, that's what I am—a murderess! (*Moves below table to* D.L.)

HUBBACK. No, no, not at all—

DORA. Please, Mrs. Hepworth, I'm sure she'll be all right.

AGATHA. Well, I 'ope so, Dora—I 'ope so.

HUBBACK. According to my calculations we should have found Miss Francis within an hour.

AGATHA (*on* L. *of* DORA). And I can't tell you, Major, how grateful I shall be if you do.

        (*A sudden burst of music from outside.*)

What's that, Dora?

DORA. It's the dancing. They're starting any minute now.

AGATHA. Well, you'd better get yourself ready, 'adn't you?

DORA. Oh, I couldn't go now, Mrs. Hepworth. Not till we know that Miss Francis is all right.

AGATHA. Of course you could! The General 'ere says he's got everything organized, so there's nothing the rest of us can do. And there's no point in you all 'anging about 'ere with long faces.

DORA. Are you sure?

AGATHA. 'course I'm sure. You go and get yourself ready.

DORA. All right. Thanks, Mrs. Hepworth!

        (DORA *runs off upstairs.*)

AGATHA. Bless her! She's a sweet girl. Don't you think so, Captain?

HUBBACK. Yes—rather!

AGATHA. I only 'ope she finds 'erself a really nice young man.

        (LEN *and* WHITTLE *come in from the beach entrance. They are both breathless and tired, and their clothes are grubby and dishevelled.*)

Have you found her?

LEN (*wearily*). Not a sign anywhere.

        (*They sink exhausted into chairs at table* L.C.; WHITTLE L. *of it,* LEN R.)

AGATHA. But there must be!

WHITTLE. We've walked around the village, and through the village, and even below the village in subterranean caves, and there's still no sign of her.

HUBBACK. What about the beach? You were supposed to begin with the beach.

WHITTLE. Oh, we tried that, too! (*He empties sand from his shoe into an ashtray.*) We asked everyone, but nobody had seen a woman answering to that description, and if they had they didn't remember. We stepped over sand castles and in and out of bathing huts, but we couldn't find her anywhere.

LEN. There was one moment when Mr. Whittle thought he recognized a body—

AGATHA. A body!

WHITTLE. Oh, the body was alive all right. It had a large sun-hat over its face, so I went up and lifted the hat to have a look.

AGATHA. Well?

WHITTLE. It was only a dirty old fisherman.

AGATHA (*pacing up to the french windows*). She must be out there somewhere! Anyhow, thank you both for what you've done.

LEN. That's all right. Well, I could do with a wash.

WHITTLE. I could do with a drink.

HUBBACK (*glancing at his watch*). Can't think what's happened to Phipps and Humbolt. They should be reporting back by now, Didn't you run into them at all?

WHITTLE. The place is so packed with people tonight that it's hard to recognize anyone. This confounded festival thing makes searching jolly difficult, you know.

HUBBACK. Better go as far as the Miramar and see if they're waiting there by mistake. Whittle, you'd better come with me.

WHITTLE. But I've only just sat down, sir.

HUBBACK. Well, now you've got to stand up again. Sorry, Whittle, but I must have a 2i/c.

WHITTLE. Couldn't I be your 2i/c back here, sir?

AGATHA (*ominously*). You don't sound very keen, Mr. Whittle.

WHITTLE. It isn't that. It's just that I'm rather tired. We've walked a long way, you know, Barrett and I.

AGATHA. Mr. Barrett's not complaining. Are you, Len?

LEN (*hurriedly*). Oh, no!

WHITTLE. He may not be up here, but he was down there.

AGATHA (*leaning across the table to him with a big smile*). I hope you're not forgetting that you're our Eagle representative.

WHITTLE. No, no! Of course I'm not!

AGATHA. And responsible for our comfort and everything—

WHITTLE. I hadn't forgotten.

AGATHA. Well, then!

WHITTLE (*rising*). All right, I'll go—I'll go! I'm quite prepared to go!

AGATHA. Good!

HUBBACK. Come on, then, Whittle! Best foot forward!

        (*He marches off, followed by a weary* WHITTLE.)

AGATHA. Aren't you going to get yourself ready then, Len?

LEN. Ready?

AGATHA. For the dancing.

LEN (*hedging*). Oh, I—I don't know if I'll go now.

AGATHA. Don't tell me you're tired.

LEN. Well, yes, I am a bit.

AGATHA. Young chap like you! You go and 'ave a wash, dear, and you'll soon be as right as rain. You can't miss a thing like this, you know.

        (*Enter* DORA *from upstairs. She is wearing the same clothes as she went up in, and is in a state of great excitement as she comes* C.)

DORA. I say, Mrs. Hepworth—

AGATHA. What is it, dear?

DORA. It's 'Rene!

AGATHA. What about her?

DORA. She's getting up!

        (*All react to this astounding piece of news.*)

AGATHA. No!

DORA. Yes! She says she's feeling a lot better and perhaps she'll get up for a while!

AGATHA. I don't believe it.

DORA. I just had to come and tell you. (*She starts to go.*)

AGATHA. No, Dora—(*Crossing to her.*)—you stay here for a while. I'll go and see to 'Rene. She'll probably need someone to lean on, and I reckon I'm the best one for that.

DORA. Oh, it's all right, Mrs. Hepworth—

AGATHA. What's the number of your room?

DORA. Forty-two, but I—

AGATHA. Right! (*To* MRS. H.) Perhaps you'd like to come and give me a hand, Audrey? I reckon the two of us are enough to put anyone back on their feet! (*Up to the archway.*)

DORA. Don't you bother, Mrs. Hubback.

MRS. H. (*rising with a smile*). It's no bother, Dora. I shall enjoy it. (*She goes up to* AGATHA.)

DORA (*astonished*). You will?

AGATHA. After you, Audrey.

MRS. H. Thank you, Agatha.

(AGATHA *follows* MRS. H. *off upstairs.*)

LEN. She's quite a character, isn't she?

DORA. Yes. I like her.

(DORA *sits* L. *of table* R.C.

There is quite a pause as they both consider what to say. From out-side we hear an orchestra playing a nostalgic Italian melody.)

LEN (*suddenly*). Dora—

DORA. Yes, Len?

LEN. Dora, you're a woman, aren't you?

DORA (*doubtfully*). Well, yes—I suppose so.

LEN. I mean for the sake of argument.

DORA. I'm a woman for the sake of anything.

LEN. Yes. Well, tell me—is there anything wrong with me?

DORA. What do you mean, Len?

(*He moves to her.*)

LEN (*with an effort*). Well, it's like this—I asked Marisa to go with me to the dancing tonight, see?

DORA. I see.

LEN. And do you know something?

DORA. What?

LEN (*in surprise*). She said no! Just like that—"No" she said.

DORA (*astonished*). Really?

LEN. Yes. I mean, I wouldn't have minded if she had already been going with some other bloke, but it wasn't like that. She just didn't want to go with me.

DORA. Perhaps she doesn't like you enough.

LEN. Well, that's why I say do you see anything wrong with me?

DORA. Oh. (*Pause.*) No.

LEN. I mean my face isn't bad, is it? 'ere, take a butcher's. (*Thrusts his face out for examination.*) It's not glamorous, I know, but it's not bad.

DORA. I think it's quite nice.

LEN (*a sudden thought*). Maybe it's the way I talk.

DORA. Oh—I like the way you talk.

LEN (*pleased*). Do you? Thanks, Dora. (*He pats her affectionately, but only as a brother.*)

DORA. That's all right.

LEN. You're a great comfort, do you know that?

DORA. Am I?

LEN. I was feeling quite miserable, but now you've cheered me up no end. Why should I care if Marisa doesn't want to go with me? She's not the only fish on the beach, is she?

DORA (*rising, hopefully*). No, Len. She's not.

LEN. You know, I think if it hadn't been for you, I'd have stayed here
moping all evening.

DORA. Would you, Len?

LEN. I certainly would. But not now—Oh, dear me, no!—I'm off
down there to get myself a glass of vino. Thanks, Dora! You're a
pal!

(LEN *goes out of the french windows.* DORA *sits disconsolately.*
AGATHA *appears almost at once from the archway.*)

AGATHA (*to* L. *of* DORA). Where's he gone?

DORA. He said I was a pal.

AGATHA. I'll give 'im pal when I see 'im!

DORA. No, Mrs. Hepworth, you mustn't say anything.

AGATHA. I know how to be subtle, you know. (*She pronounces the "b" in*
subtle.)

DORA. He's just not interested.

AGATHA. You need more confidence, my girl. No good going into
battle with that sort of attitude.

DORA. I'm not going into battle.

AGATHA. Yes, you are! It may not be much of an offensive yet, but
you're going into battle all right. You should 'ave gone with 'im.

DORA. But he didn't ask me.

AGATHA. Then you should 'ave asked him.

DORA. I couldn't do that.

AGATHA. Why not? (*Pulling* DORA *to her feet.*) Come on—you'll 'ave
to go down there and find him!

DORA. What? I couldn't!

AGATHA. No such word. Come on, let's 'ave you changed into your
dress!

DORA (*as they go*). But what about Rene?

AGATHA. She's all right. Audrey's looking after her.

(*They go upstairs.* HUBBACK *marches in through the french*
windows to C., *followed by an even more weary* WHITTLE, *who*
subsides into the chair R. *of table* L.C.)

HUBBACK. Can't think what's happened to the blighters! Both seemed
reliable chaps. Not at all the sort to fall by the wayside.

WHITTLE. Maybe they've found a clue and are following it up.

HUBBACK (*pacing downstage to* D.R.). Then they should have reported to
me. They could have sent a runner. Get some of these chaps back
into uniform and I'd soon make them jump!

WHITTLE. Well, there's nothing else you can do, sir. May as well settle
down here and wait.

HUBBACK. H'm. Perhaps you're right. How about a drink?

WHITTLE. A good idea, sir.

HUBBACK (*calling off*). Mario! Two large whiskies, please. Ice and plenty of soda.

> (HUBBACK *wanders up to the archway and then crosses above* WHITTLE *to* L. *of table* L.C.)

I wonder where the wife's got to. Probably having her bath. She's a woman of routine, Whittle. Always likes her bath at the same time, that sort of thing.

WHITTLE. As a military man that should appeal to you.

HUBBACK. Oh, yes—no complaints about that. I like her to have a bath occasionally. (*Sits* L. *of table* L.C.) I mean I'm always sure of a quiet drink while she's having it. You ever think of getting married, Whittle?

WHITTLE. No, thank you, sir.

> (MARISA *comes in with drinks, dressed to go dancing.*)

MARISA. Your drinks.

HUBBACK. Thought you'd have gone to the dancing, Marisa.

MARISA. I am just going. You are coming for a dance, Signor?

HUBBACK. Oh, you mustn't tempt me!

> (*Outside we hear the crackle of fireworks.*)

MARISA. Listen—the fireworks are starting.

HUBBACK. The fireworks will be starting all right if I go out there! What shall I do, Whittle?

WHITTLE. Your wife will be out of her bath very soon.

HUBBACK. Too risky, you think?

WHITTLE. Much too risky, sir.

HUBBACK. Pity. I'd love to, m'dear, but Whittle's right. (*Turning to* WHITTLE.) Oh, no harm in one dance, surely? I mean, I ought to keep an eye out for Miss Francis. If I mingle with the crowd a bit I may spot her. Come along, my dear! All in the line of duty!

> (MARIA *and* HUBBACK *go out through the french windows.* WHITTLE *settles himself more comfortably as* AGATHA *comes in from upstairs.*)

AGATHA. Oh, you're back, Mr. Whittle!

WHITTLE (*nervously*). Er—yes.

AGATHA. Did you find those men you went to look for?

WHITTLE. No. They haven't returned yet.

AGATHA. Where's the General?

WHITTLE. He's doing a little reconnaissance.

> (*There is a pause as* AGATHA *comes across and regards* MR. WHITTLE. *He sinks a little lower in his chair.*)

AGATHA. You do look comfortable, Mr. Whittle.

WHITTLE. I am, rather.

AGATHA. I expect you're tired, aren't you?

WHITTLE. I am a bit.

AGATHA. You could do with a nice long rest.

WHITTLE. Yes, I could.

AGATHA (*loudly*). That's a pity, because now you've got to start again!

WHITTLE (*wearily*). Have I?

AGATHA. You certainly 'ave! You're our Eagle representative, aren't you?

WHITTLE. Yes, but—

AGATHA. Then it's your responsibility. Come on! (*Pulls him to his feet.*)

WHITTLE. Couldn't we wait just a little longer?

AGATHA (*dragging him towards the french windows*). We're going to find my sister if we 'ave to go on searching all night.

WHITTLE. Where are we likely to find her at this time?

AGATHA. If I know her, she'll be down there watching the dancing. She never could resist a crowd.

WHITTLE. We'll never find her amongst all that lot.

AGATHA. Then we'll keep on trying. And if you're very good, Mr. Whittle, and be'ave yourself—

WHITTLE. Yes, Mrs. Hepworth?

AGATHA. You can 'ave one dance—with me!

> (AGATHA *drags* WHITTLE *out through the french windows. Outside we can hear the crackle of fireworks and gay Italian music.*)

> (*After a moment* FIONA *comes in by the main entrance. She has caught the sun and is very red. She looks around the empty room and then goes back to the door and calls off.*)

FIONA. It's all right—come on in!

> (MR. MALLET *follows her in, looking rather sheepish.*)

(*Moving to* C.) There, you see! What did I tell you? I bet nobody's missed us at all. I don't know what you were worrying about.

> (*She sits with a sigh* L. *of table* R.C. MALLET *to* R. *of table* R.C.)

Oh, we 'ad a nice day, didn't we, Jack?

MALLET. Yes, lovely.

FIONA. I wonder what the others have been doing.

MALLET. Playing cricket, I expect.

> (*They both laugh at this.*)

FIONA. You know, I didn' expect to enjoy myself out 'ere.

MALLET. Then why did you come?

FIONA. It was Agatha. She said it would be good for me. I don't know what she meant. We usually go to Eastcliffe. Have you ever been there?

MALLET. No. (*Pause.*) Last year I went pony-trekking. It was quite enjoyable.

FIONA. I rode a horse once. I didn't care for it, really. I certainly wouldn't like a fortnight with my backside bobbing up and down.

MALLET. Twelve of us went from the bank.

FIONA. One year we went to one of those holiday camps.

MALLET. You ride from place to place, you know.

FIONA. Oh, it was ever so nice. There's so much to do there that you hardly have time to see the sea. On the last night—I shall never forget it—we all stood round in a ring and held hands and sang "Auld Lang Syne". The tears simply poured down my face! Oh, it was lovely!

MALLET. Of course, you have to look after your own horse.

(Pause.)

FIONA. You don't suppose they've all got lost or something, do you?

MALLET. I shouldn't think so.

FIONA. Be funny, wouldn't it, if they had and we had to go out and search for them!

(DORA comes in from upstairs.)

Hullo, dear.

DORA *(in great excitement at seeing her)*. Miss Francis. You're back! *(She rushes down to L. of FIONA.)*

FIONA *(puzzled)*. What, dear?

(DORA rushes across and embraces her. FIONA and MALLET are rather surprised at this somewhat emotional greeting.)

DORA. Oh, it is good to see you again!

FIONA. Well, thank you, dear. That's very nice of you. Isn't that nice, Jack?

DORA. And it was you who did it, eh, Mr. Mallet?

MALLET. I beg your pardon?

DORA. All on your own you did it?

MALLET. I'm not quite sure what—

DORA. Made all the rest of them look foolish anyhow.

MALLET. Rest of who?

DORA. Just wait till you tell them all. I can't wait to see their faces!

MALLET. What am I going to tell them all?

DORA. About you and Miss Francis, of course! *(Embraces FIONA again.)* Oh, I am glad to see you!

FIONA. Perhaps you'd like to sit down for a bit, dear? It's been a very hot day. Would you like a glass of water?

(MALLET, unnoticed, goes off for a glass of water D.R.)

DORA. No, thanks. I'm fine. But what about you? You must be worn out—I mean, the shock and everything. It must have been terrible! Were you frightened?

FIONA *(completely bewildered)*. Frightened? No, dear.

DORA. I think you're ever so brave!

FIONA. Are you sure you're all right, dear?

DORA. Me? Of course I am. What do you mean?

FIONA. Oh, nothing! (*Changing the subject deliberately.*) I thought you'd be down there at the dancing.

DORA. Well, I was going, but I decided not.

FIONA. Why?

DORA. Oh—I dunno.

FIONA (*gently*). Didn't he ask you to go?

DORA (*after a pause*). No. I think I shall go on being a spinster all my life.

FIONA. Of course you won't. Take my word for it. I used to think that.

> (*A pause, then* DORA *realizes what* FIONA *has said.*)

DORA. What do you mean? Don't—don't you think it any longer? You mean—you mean you and Mr. Mallet—?

FIONA. S'sh! Nothing definite, dear. But you never know. He's really quite nice. (*Turns to find* MALLET *has gone.*) Jack—Jack! Here, where have you got to?

> (*She goes off in search of* MALLET D.R. DORA *laughs, then with sudden decision runs off upstairs.*
>
> WHITTLE, AGATHA *and* LEN *come in from the french windows.* AGATHA *to* C. WHITTLE *sinks into chair* R. *of table* L.C.; LEN *remains downstage of french windows.*)

WHITTLE. No sign of her anywhere. I said it was hopeless in that crowd.

AGATHA. You're the one who's hopeless, Mr. Whittle. You're about as bad at searching as you are at dancing.

WHITTLE. I did my best.

LEN. Blimey, you don't mean you actually got him on his feet, Mrs. Hepworth?

AGATHA. He was on my feet most of the time.

WHITTLE. Well, I said it would be better if I led!

AGATHA. Well, I suppose there's nothing else we can do tonight. 'eaven knows I shan't sleep a wink! The police say they're doing all they can. But first thing in the morning—you listening, Whittle!— first thing in the morning we're off again.

WHITTLE (*wearily*). Yes, Mrs. Hepworth. Anything you say.

AGATHA. You ought to be glad you're earning your money for once instead of sitting on your bottom in the sunshine. (*Moves upstage towards the archway.*)

WHITTLE. Nothing I should hate more.

> (HUBBACK *comes in from the french windows. He is red-faced and rather breathless. He does not at first see* AGATHA *as he comes to above table* L.C.)

HUBBACK. I say, Whittle, I'm not as fit as I was, y'know. A couple of dances and I'm quite breathless.

AGATHA (*moving downstage*). You been dancing, Major?

HUBBACK. Thought I might pick up a few clues.

AGATHA. And did you?

HUBBACK. Er—no. Anything to report, Whittle?

WHITTLE. No, sir, not a thing.

HUBBACK. Pity. No sign of Humbolt and Phipps?

WHITTLE. I think they must have deserted, sir.

HUBBACK. Possibly, possibly. Still, there were some good men under them. Bound to be someone who could take over.

AGATHA. Those your search parties, Colonel?

HUBBACK. Brigadier, yes. Afraid they appear to have got lost. (*To* L. *of* AGATHA *at* C.) Still, never say die. Bound to turn up soon. Anyone seen my wife, by the way?

WHITTLE. Why? Are you looking for her?

HUBBACK. Er—well, not exactly looking, y'know. Just wondered. Just wondered. Thought she might have been looking for me, actually.

AGATHA. You been having a good time then, General?

HUBBACK. Er—Brigadier. Time you learned my rank, y'know. Chopping and changing. Bad for discipline.

AGATHA. Oh, I am sorry, luv.

(MRS. HUBBACK *comes in from upstairs.*)

HUBBACK (*crossing to her*). Ah! I was just coming to look for you, m' dear.

MRS. H. Why do you say that, Charles? You know perfectly well it isn't true. I just came down for my aspirins. Poor Irene has a bit of a headache.

HUBBACK. Irene?

AGATHA. Dora's friend.

HUBBACK. Oh—Rene!

MRS. H. Her name is Irene and she's a very sweet girl. Charles, you're looking rather flushed.

HUBBACK. Yes. I've been running.

MRS. H. Why? Was somebody chasing you? I should have thought you'd had enough exercise for one night.

HUBBACK. What do you mean?

MRS. H. It must be years since you danced quite so energetically.

HUBBACK. Danced?

MRS. H. Irene's room looks out over the square, you know. I've been sitting with her. We've had a wonderful time watching you all.

HUBBACK (*subsiding*). Oh, lord!

MRS. H. By the way, Charles, we must be up bright and early, in the morning.

HUBBACK. Must we?

MRS. H. Yes. You see, Irene thinks she'll be all right to go out tomorrow. Well, the poor girl's only got until Friday, and I'm determined she's going to enjoy every minute of it. (*She looks across at*
AGATHA.) Right, Agatha?

AGATHA (*beaming*). Right, Audrey!

(*Exit* MRS. H. *upstairs.* HUBBACK *goggles.*)

HUBBACK. What's happened to her? She must have gone mad! I'll be
back in a minute. (*Making for the exit.*) Audrey! Here, I say—
Audrey! Audrey!

(*Exit* HUBBACK.)

AGATHA. Well, I 'ope Rene does get out tomorrow. Be a shame to go
back home without seeing the sea at all.

WHITTLE. That's a matter of opinion.

AGATHA. You know, you're as bad as that sister of mine. (*To french
windows.*) Oh, dear, I wonder where she can be. She's probably
lying ill and lonely somewhere just calling out for me.

FIONA (*off*). Is that you, Agatha?

(*They all freeze.*)

AGATHA (*hushed*). What was that?

WHITTLE. Someone calling out for you.

AGATHA. It sounded like her.

LEN. Who? Your sister?

AGATHA. Yes. It was her voice.

WHITTLE. It couldn't have been.

AGATHA. I tell you it was. Or maybe I only imagined it. Maybe she's
dead and she's come back to 'aunt me for my wickedness!

(FIONA *comes in* D.R.)

FIONA. No, Agatha. I'm over 'ere.

(AGATHA *turns and looks at her. They move slowly towards each
other to meet at* C.)

AGATHA (*stunned*). You're . . . not dead, then?

FIONA. No, Agatha, of course I'm not.

AGATHA (*loudly*). Well, you ought to be ashamed of yourself!

LEN (*moving* D.L.). Are you all right, Miss Francis?

FIONA. Oh, yes, I'm quite all right, thank you.

AGATHA (*the voice of thunder*). Fiona Francis, where 'ave you been?

FIONA. Well, first of all I sat on the beach.

AGATHA. You sat on the beach! We were all going mad with worry
and you sat on the beach!

FIONA. It was such a lovely afternoon.

AGATHA. I'll give you a lovely afternoon.

FIONA. Then I went for a paddle. I tucked up my dress and walked for miles. (*Innocently.*) You haven't all been looking for me, have you?

AGATHA. Not only us—the police, the coast guard, the fishermen—everyone bar the camel corps!

WHITTLE (*in a weary voice*). Mr. Barrett and I spent the whole afternoon on the beach.

FIONA. Oh, yes—I saw you going by.

AGATHA. You saw them? (*Vesuvius in eruption is as nothing to* AGATHA *at this moment.*)

FIONA. Yes, I didn't like to call out. They looked so busy.

AGATHA. They were busy all right—looking for you!

FIONA. Well, I never!

AGATHA. We could all have been enjoying ourselves, but thanks to you we've been carrying on like a lot of bloomin' bloodhounds! (*Paces away to below table* R.C.)

FIONA. But I didn't know you'd be worried.

WHITTLE. Mrs. Hepworth thought you might be dead. She was very upset.

FIONA (*turning to* AGATHA, *amazed*). She was?

WHITTLE. Yes.

FIONA. Were you, Agatha?

AGATHA (*her back to* FIONA). Of course I wasn't! I just didn't want a sister of mine making a spectacle of 'erself. (*Turning and pounding up to* R. *of* FIONA.) There's a time and place to die, and the time isn't now and the place isn't 'ere!

FIONA. Well, I did think of telephoning you.

AGATHA. You surprise me.

FIONA. But then I said to Jack, I said, "I know Agatha, and she won't worry".

AGATHA. You said to 'oo?

FIONA. Jack. Oh, dear! I've left him in there. (*To door* D.R.) Come on in, Jack. Everyone's in here.

(MR. MALLET *comes in.*)

You remember Mr. Mallet, Agatha.

AGATHA. Yes, I'm afraid I do. You seem to spend your time getting lost, Mr. Mallet.

MALLET. Oh, we weren't lost! Were we, Fiona?

FIONA. No, of course we weren't, Jack.

AGATHA (*to* D.R.C.). Fiona? Jack? What's all this?

FIONA. That's his name, Agatha.

AGATHA. I see. So all the time we were going mad with worry, thinking what an 'orrible end you might 'ave come to, you were busy getting on to Christian-name terms with Marco Polo!

FIONA. His name isn't Marco Polo. It's Jack.

AGATHA. You ought to be ashamed of yourself.

FIONA. You said I might sit on the beach and meet my dream man. Well, I did and I have! (*She takes* MALLET'*s arm.*)

AGATHA (*subsiding into the chair* L. *of table* R.C.). Oh, blimey!
　　　　(DORA *appears from upstairs. She is wearing an attractive dress, and looks very pretty. They all gaze at her in admiration. Even* LEN *is struck by her appearance.*)

FIONA. Oh, doesn't she look lovely!

AGATHA. Yes, doesn't she?

DORA. I thought I'd just pop down to the dancing for a while. See you all later!
　　　　(*Without so much as a sideways glance at* LEN *she proceeds to the french windows.* LEN *gazes in dumb admiration, crosses to* C. *in a dream and follows her off without a word.*)

FIONA. How about you and me going for a dance, Jack?

MALLET. Anything you say, Fiona.
　　　　(FIONA *and* MALLET *cross towards the french windows.*)

AGATHA (*rising*). Now mind you two don't go astray again!

FIONA (*with a giggle*). I don't care if I do!

AGATHA. Now, then! You're not nineteen, you know. Anyone would fancy you were thinking of getting married.

FIONA. Don't you be so sure that I'm not!
　　　　(FIONA *and* MALLET *go out by the french windows.*
　　　　AGATHA *looks around and sees* WHITTLE *sitting comfortably in his chair. She crosses slowly towards him with a beaming smile. He smiles back briefly, then begins to feel uncomfortable. He glances around the room and realizes with horror that he is alone with her.*)

WHITTLE (*with sudden realization*). Oh, no!
　　　　He is attempting to make his escape as

THE CURTAIN FALLS.

PROPERTY PLOT

ACT ONE

Set:

Vase (*table* R.C.)
Italian magazines (*Seat* U.C.)
Bathing-towel ⎫ (HUBBACK.
Bathing-trunks ⎬ *Off* R.)
Flowers (MARISA. *Off* R.)
Two tea trays (MARISA. *Off* R.)
On each:
    Two cups and saucers
    Two teaspoons
    Teapot
    Milk jug
    Sugar in packets
    Plate of biscuits
Week-end case (AGATHA. *Off* R.)
Handbag (AGATHA. *Off* R.)
In it:
    Italian phrase-book
    Passport
    Rail tickets
    Itinerary
    Travel brochure
    Pen
Two suitcases ⎫
One travelling grip ⎪
One brown paper parcel ⎬ (FIONA. *Off* R.)
One carrier bag ⎪
One umbrella ⎭

Handbag (FIONA. *Off* R.)
In it:
    Pink form
    Travel sickness pills
    Pen
Panama hat (HUBBACK. *Off* R.)
Sunglasses (MRS. HUBBACK. *Off* R.)
Suitcase (LEN. *Off* R.)
Grip (LEN. *Off* R.)
Travel brochure (FIONA. *Off* R.)
Picture postcards (AGATHA. *Off* R.)
Bottle of sun-oil (DORA. *Off* R.)
Bathing-towel (DORA. *Off* R.)
Orange drink on tray (MARISA. *Off* R.)
Orange drink on tray with soda syphon (MARISA. *Off* R.)
English newspapers (HUBBACK. *Off* R.)

Personal:

Itinerary, papers, etc. (MALLET)
Handkerchief (WHITTLE)
Official papers (WHITTLE)

ACT TWO

Set:

Magazines on table D.R.
Two dirty cups and saucers (*Table* R.C.)
Two plates with bits of roll (*Table* R.C.)
Tray (*Table* R.C.)
One dirty cup and saucer (*Table* L.C.)
Flowers in vase (MARISA. *Off* R.)
Duster (MARISA. *Off* R.)
Book (MRS. H. *Off* R.)
Camera (HUBBACK. *Off* R.)
Straw hat for Fiona (AGATHA. *Off* R.)
Beach bag (AGATHA. *Off* R.)
In it:
    Tube of shaving-cream

    Inflatable beach ball
    Knitting
Brownie camera (MARISA. *Off* R.)
Glass of water (MARISA. *Off* R.)
Orange drink (DORA. *Off* R.)
Cricket bat (AGATHA. *Off* R.)
Sweater (Whittle. *Off* L.)
Orange drink (MARISA. *Off* R.)
Small tray (MARISA. *Off* R.)
On it:
    One pink gin
    One sherry

Personal:

Dark glasses (AGATHA)
Straw hat (AGATHA)